Culture and the Classroom

CURRICULUM STUDIES

General Editor: David Jenkins

Culture and the Classroom

John Reynolds and **Malcolm Skilbeck**

Open Books
London

First published in 1976 by Open Books Publishing Limited, 87-89
Shaftesbury Avenue, LONDON WIV 7AD

© John Reynolds and Malcolm Skilbeck 1976
Hardback: ISBN   0 7291 0056 1
Paperback: ISBN   0 7291 0051 0

Filmset in Linotron 11 pt Baskerville by
G. A. Pindar & Son Ltd, Scarborough, N. Yorkshire
Printed in Great Britain by The Pitman Press, Bath

Contents

Acknowledgements

The authors and publishers would like to thank the following for permission to use material reproduced in this book: The Centre for Applied Research in Education, University of East Anglia, for the extract from Donald Hamingson (ed.), *Towards Judgement* (1973); Harcourt, Brace and World for the extracts from Smith, Stanley and Shores, *Fundamentals of Curriculum Development* (1957); Harvard University Press for extracts from Jerome Bruner, *Toward a Theory of Instruction* (1966); The Schools Council for the diagram on the curriculum strategy of the Schools Council Geography 14-18 Project; Ward Lock Ltd for extracts from Eric Midwinter, *Projections and the Social Environment* (1972).

Editor's introduction

Curriculum studies is one of the growth points in education today. In essence it takes as problematic what should be planned, taught and learned in our schools. It is a central and centralising study organised around the choices facing the practitioner. It can be gritty and ragged about the edges, lacking the settled apparatus of other disciplines in education, but it aspires to being *usable*. Curriculum studies is a recognition of the needs felt by practitioners for better ways of describing, explaining and justifying what goes on in educational programmes. The question *What ought we to be teaching in our schools?* is a more complex one than appears at first glance: this series explores the underlying complexities.

There are perhaps two major reasons for the present upsurge of interest in curriculum theory and practice. The first is that we have just completed in British education the first cycle of the curriculum reform movement (a cycle brought to an end by the current financial stringency); this movement brought to the surface a number of pressing issues — it was never simply a question of updating the knowledge component. There have been two main trends in the analysis of the 'curriculum reform' phenomenon. The first stresses the movement as an attempt to *institutionalise* the whole process of curriculum change and seeks to explore the full implications of making the curriculum into a legitimate object of social policy. The second points to the 'grass roots' image of reform and characterises the curriculum reform movement in terms of the emergence of 'curriculum entrepreneurs', first-generation project directors who backed hunches derived from their own experience. Both accounts raise problems. The first suggests that the principal issue is a boundary dispute over professional autonomy between administrators and teachers. The second invites us to view the curriculum reform movement as a free enterprise system in which change agents invent and disseminate classroom novelty in the teeth of an inadequate infrastructure for planned change. But neither of these 'social movement' perspectives is much help in generating the kind of research tradition that would allow us to explore the conflicting premisses behind alternative proposals.

The second reason for the upsurge in interest to some extent complements the first. I refer to the emergence of a 'community of discourse' in the universities, in the schools, in the colleges of education and the teachers' centres, which have become seriously interested in curriculum as an area of study. This is not to suggest that the 'practical' reform movement spawned a derivative 'theoretical' literature, for the same people were frequently involved in both. Indeed such an overlap is wholly appropriate given the aspiration of curriculum studies to be a theory about practice – and a practitioners' theory. One sign of the emerging 'community of discourse' has been the proliferation of courses in curriculum, both in-service and as part of initial training.

This series is an attempt to explore the main issues likely to recur in curriculum studies courses. Its authors have all been involved directly in curriculum reform, either as teachers, project members or evaluators. All are familiar with the world of the classroom. Most have many years of teaching experience (in my own case over eight in a South Wales comprehensive school) and all are currently involved in preparing and teaching curriculum studies in teacher education.

Although part of a series, each book is capable of standing on its own. All have end-of-chapter summaries, and suggestions for further reading.

This particular volume, *Culture and the Classroom,* was written by John Reynolds and Malcolm Skilbeck. John Reynolds is lecturing in curriculum studies at Lancaster University following a period during which he was at the School of Education at the University of Bristol, and Director of the Schools Council Geography 14-18 Project. Malcolm Skilbeck was also at Bristol as Senior Tutor in the Advanced Studies Division before moving to the New University of Ulster as Professor of Education and Director of the Education Centre where he was responsible for the major emerging institution of teacher education in Northern Ireland. Professor Skilbeck was actively involved in a number of curriculum projects, including one in social and community education, supported by the Rowntree Trust. He has very recently moved back to his native Australia to take up the newly created post of Director of the National Curriculum Development Centre.

Culture and the Curriculum explores the complex relationship between culture, the definition of which is treated as problematic, and curriculum provision. One of the issues discussed is how teachers can play an active role in a curriculum that is inevitably in a process of continual social reconstruction, rather than seeing themselves as either preservers of a culture that must somehow be handed on intact, or simply responding to change.

David Jenkins

1 CULTURAL PERSPECTIVES ON CURRICULUM: THREE EXEMPLARS

The fish will be the last to discover water

To see curriculum in terms of culture is to consider the usually implicit relationship between schooling and the basic conceptions and expectations in the society that sponsors it. In short, this book is about what the connection is and ought to be between the forms of experiencing promoted in schools and those prevailing outside them. More particularly, it is to question how the selection and structuring of experience in schools reflects and shapes the established ways of sharing, regulating and communicating about life that men evolve through common forms of expression, symbols and systems of action; that is to say, culture.

Unfortunately, the idea of culture is associated with either 'high culture' (the arts) or nineteenth century anthropology (and an interest in exotic artefacts). The following passage may suggest how an analytic general concept of culture can be distinguished from narrower or blunter uses, so as to focus on how men develop patterns of meaning and significance.

A SWEET AND SOUR SHAGGY DOG STORY
A couple have returned from holiday with the sad story of how their pet poodle was accidentally cooked as their main dish in a Chinese restaurant in Hongkong. Hans and

Erna W. from Zurich, whose 'tale' appears in a Swiss newspaper which says they have asked for their full names not to be published because of the emotional shock they have undergone, said they had taken their poodle Rosa along with them to an evening meal.

They asked a waiter over to their table and pointed to the poodle while they made eating motions, to show that they wanted it to be fed. There was some difficulty communicating with the waiter they said, but eventually he took Rosa off into the kitchen under his arm. About an hour later he came back with their main dish. When they picked up the silver lid they found their poodle roasted inside, garnished with pepper sauce and bamboo shoots. The couple said they suffered from a mild nervous collapse and did not eat the dog. They returned to Zurich immediately.

(*The Guardian*, 21 August 1971)

We can respond to the story at three main levels of consciousness. First, we can react either to its concrete content – for example, 'Ugh! Poor dog!' – or by sympathising with the waiter. The content may immediately fit into our assumptions about the sentimentality and naivety of affluent Europeans, or about the uncivilised customs of non-Europeans. We can use cultural stereotypes to interpret the experience. At a second level of consciousness, we may respond in a more detached reflective way. We can distance the content of the story by recourse to some simple form of explanation, to the effect that people see things differently. Our interpretation of the surface content of the story can be mediated by an implicit 'theory' that culture varies with geographical or social position. We can go on to link this generalisation with the analysis of people's differing 'life styles', their 'world views', and related social and economic organisation.

This brings us into a third level of consciousness, in which

2

we can interpret the story by thinking about the participants' structure of consciousness. We could interpose a more explicit theory of how culture is constituted by three main elements: symbolic forms which select and coordinate people's individual experience (in this case, crude symbolic forms, gesture and mime); conventions of usage developed through interaction within social groups (hence the cultural misinterpretation which led to Rosa's demise); and systems of beliefs, values and action.

We shall draw particularly on this third approach to culture. It is sometimes called the semiotic approach to culture, because its central concern is the process by which patterns of meaning and significance in people's lives develop, how they are selected, bounded and coded. It differs in emphasis from many other views of culture and education which deal rather more with how the outcomes of culture are differentiated; either vertically (for example, into 'high' and working class culture) or horizontally, between regions and peoples. We can illustrate the point by referring again to the fate of Rosa. We chose the passage to avoid the dulling effect that the familiarity of reciprocated meanings in everyday life has on our sensitivity to culture. When meanings in interactions between people do not interlock, we tend to attribute this to their obtuseness, or antagonism, or to 'failure in communication'. But to see these situations in terms of culture is to recognise that the words or other symbols (numbers, diagrams or images, etc.) that we use in teaching and ordinary life are sophisticated ways of 'pointing' to and selecting aspects of experience. Their capacity to focus effectively on experience in complex situations, hence to share it and prompt predictable actions, may be as uncertain in the classroom as in a Chinese reataurant.

Many teachers try to introduce children to the analysis of issues such as moral values, 'good taste', social policy, etc. Often they abandon the attempt on failing to find symbols which provide adequate common foci in experience for chil-

3

dren to look honestly at the complexity of the issues. This can be partly explained in psychological terms, by showing that concepts like 'fairness', 'beauty', 'democracy', etc., are more abstract than they seem, and that children only gradually learn to use them meaningfully. But it is also a question of the conceptions and expectations that both teachers and children bring into the classroom from the surrounding culture. We assume that the curriculum is for the transmission of skills and information, and, more recently, techniques of investigation; and the timetable is organised accordingly. Teachers who try to depart from this pattern of expectations – for example, science teachers who look at cultural problems such as the relation between research and social policy, as in the correlation between lung cancer and smoking – may seem to depart from reality. They may be as misunderstood as Hans and Erna W.

There is nothing new in the view that schools should look more systematically at the relation between curriculum and culture. In chapter 2 we shall consider why the view has had relatively little effect on school practice. But first we can consider three differing approaches to curriculum development which have explicitly and cogently used the idea of culture.

(1) Smith, Stanley and Shores (1957) – Cultural diagnosis and the idea of a common culture core curriculum

Over twenty years ago Smith, Stanley and Shores wrote what is still one of the most concise and lucid analyses of basic ideas in curriculum development. They began as follows:

The people of every society are confronted by the problem of inducting the immature members into their culture, that is, into the ways of the group. The individual at birth is a cultural barbarian, in that he has none of the habits, ideas, attitudes and skills characterizing the adult

4

members of society. . .

In primitive societies the individual acquires these learnings informally from association with adults in their daily activities . . . In literate societies instruction in group ways becomes partly a specialized function. An institution – the school – is created. A sequence of potential experiences is set up in the school for the purpose of disciplining children and youth in group ways of thinking and acting. This set of experiences is referred to as the *curriculum*. . .

To understand the structure and function of the curriculum it is necessary to understand what is meant by culture, what the essential elements of a culture are. . .

A culture is the fabric of ideas, ideals, beliefs, skills, tools, aesthetic objects, methods of thinking, customs and institutions into which each member of society is born. The way individuals make a living, the games they play, the stories they tell. . .

Smith, Stanley and Shores went on to develop the following position. Culture can be analysed into three elements. (1) *Universal* elements accepted by all members of the society; conventions about language, conduct, work, dress, that everyone expects of their children. (2) *Special* cultural elements (or 'subcultures') such as vocational skills, in farming, industry, etc.; and also the customs and expertise vested in particular social groupings, such as folk culture, youth culture, 'high' culture. (3) *Alternative* cultural elements; that is to say, ways of thinking and doing that diverge from the practice of recognised social groups, and which often represent innovations and departures from universal and specialist cultures. For example, we currently talk about a 'counter culture' in which people dissatisfied with the dominant industrial culture have established communes or are trying to live by ecologically-balanced forms of farming.

The well-being of both the individual and the community depends on a minimal integration of the elements of culture;

5

but in our society (so Smith, Stanley and Shores argue) this integration is subject to increasing stress. Education, therefore, has a key role to play in helping people to develop their culture in response to inevitable social change. To do this, schools must provide a common educational core to sustain the 'fundamental universals, or cultural core, such as values, sentiments, knowledge and skills that provide society with stability and vitality. . .'

But the most important part of the argument is this. Although the purpose of the core cultural element in the curriculum is to develop cultural unity and stability, it cannot do so by 'transmitting' current values and beliefs *as they stand*; and hence cannot do so by reproducing established ways of organising the curriculum in terms of 'subjects' (as in most of our secondary schools) or 'activities' (as in many of our primary schools). Rather, the core curriculum must be structured in terms of 'broad social problems and themes of social living' – for example, 'the protection and conservation of life, property and natural resources'. Equally significantly, the core curriculum is intended to develop children's ability to *reinterpret* culture – which is neither to accept it unreflectively, nor to criticise it without coming to understand its complex fabric and funded wisdom. Hence the core curriculum must provide children with learning experience to develop both the intellectual and social skills to resolve broad cultural problems. This demands considerable reorganisation of curricula, so that existing 'subjects' and methods can be used as resources rather than as determinants.

(2) Bruner (1966) – Man: A Course of Study

At the level of overall curriculum planning, the use of the idea of culture by Smith, Stanley and Shores has great cogency. But the individual school and teacher found it difficult to translate it into actual teaching materials and strategies. It was much easier and less time consuming to use

6

existing textbooks and subject structures. In the United States in the 1960s it seemed clear that if curriculum activities about culture and broad social problems were to be made interesting and intellectually exacting for children, then curriculum construction could not be left entirely to teachers with limited time and resources. The most notable response to this need was the work of a team of scholars and teachers directed by Peter Dow and advised by the distinguished psychologist, Jerome Bruner.

It is impossible to do full justice to the MACOS (Man: A Course of Study) team's ideas except through experience of the full range of materials and audiovisual support. They are very expensive and entail a preparatory training course. But the three extracts that follow (from *Toward a Theory of Instruction* (Bruner 1966), pp. 75-6, 87-8, 92-3, respectively) help to illustrate how the idea of culture was articulated in its teaching materials and strategies.

(1) STRUCTURE OF THE COURSE

The content of the course is man: his nature as a species, the forces that shaped and continue to shape his humanity. Three questions recur throughout:

What is human about human beings?

How did they get that way?

How can they be made more so?

We seek exercises and materials through which our pupils can learn wherein man is distinctive in his adaptation to the world, and wherein there is discernible continuity between him and his animal forebears. For man represents that crucial point in evolution where adaptation is achieved by the vehicle of culture . . .

In pursuit of our questions we proceed to explore five subjects, each closely associated with the evolution of man as a species, each defining at once the distinctiveness of man and his potentiality for further evolution. The five great humanising forces are (1) language, (2) tool making,

(3) social organisation, (4) the management of man's prolonged childhood, and (5) man's urge to explain his world (i.e. his 'world view').

(2) WORLD VIEW

[The fifth theme in the course] is concerned with man's drive to explain and represent his world . . .

The very essence of being human lies in the use of symbols. We do not know what the hierarchy of primacy is among speech, song, dance, and drawing, but, whichever came first, as soon as it stood for something else than the act itself, man was born; and as soon as it caught on with another man, culture was born; as soon as there were two symbols, a system was born. A dance, a song, a painting, and a narrative can all symbolise the same thing. They do so differently . . .

We have selected, for our starting point, two hunting-gathering societies – Eskimo and Bushman – to show what the life experience of hunting peoples is. From the scrutiny of the myths of these groups, it is immediately clear that you can tell a society by its narratives. The ecology, the economy, the social structure, the tasks of men and women, and their fears and anxieties are reflected in the stories, and in a way that the children can handle. One good example of Eskimo narrative or Eskimo poetry, if skilfully handled in class, can show the child that the problems of an Eskimo are like our problems: to cope with his environment, to cope with his fellow men, and to cope with himself.

(3) TEACHING STRATEGIES

The most persistent problem in teaching social studies is to rescue the phenomena of social life from familiarity, without at the same time making it all seem 'primitive' and bizarre. Four techniques are proving particularly useful in achieving this end. The first is *contrast* . . . The second is *the stimulation and use of informed guessing, hypothesis making, conjectural procedures.* The third is *participation* – particularly by the use of games that incorporate the formal properties of the phenomena for which the game is an analogue. The fourth is the ancient approach of *stimulating self-consciousness.* We believe there is a learnable strategy for discovering one's unspoken notions, one's unstated ways of approaching things.

One of the initial criticisms made of this approach was that it might over-emphasise how children come to understand man and culture in rational, intellectual terms; that it might neglect the role of emotion and imagination, myth and fantasy, in children's responses. But Bruner would be the first to stress their importance in culture. However, he would also argue that the separation of thought and feeling, of the cognitive and affective, can be misleading. As we attend to feelings, such as anger, fear, jealousy, etc., we become conscious of what they are directed at; and to some extent we transform them and bring them under control. Consider, for example, the MACOS project's suggestions about learning experience following a film on an Eskimo hunt for caribou:

After the film is over, give the children a chance to express their reactions in any one of several ways: class or small group discussion; small group role-play of the entire hunt; illustration of key scenes from the film, or creative writing. Here are some questions which could help the children reflect on and discuss their reactions to the film:
Have you ever seen or experienced anything else that made you feel the same way? . . . perhaps something you saw on television or film?
Is your reaction to the killing of the caribou connected with other feelings about violence or cruelty or anything else?
How are we taught that certain things are cruel?

How do you feel if you see a grown-up or an older child hit a young child?

What things do we do which the Eskimos might consider unnecessarily cruel or violent?

(Extract from MACOS, Notes for Teachers)

In short, Man: A Course of Study is an outstanding repository of generative curriculum ideas. Our concern is its exemplification of the idea of culture. At the price of simplification, we can summarise that exemplification as follows. Both the *content* of the course and the recommended learning *process* embody a powerful and coherent vision of men (and pupils) as 'meaning makers'. Through the medium of culture they are capable of extraordinary achievements of cooperation, expressiveness, inventiveness and persistence. In developing this vision of man and culture, MACOS shows the value of sophisticated ideas from the social sciences.

In doing so, it can provide an intellectual stimulus to primary schools where an uncritical child-centred approach can induce teachers to shun abstract, probing approaches to people's ideas and values. Though the broad target of the course was the middle school range, younger children can respond thoughtfully to its use of the unfamiliar and evocative to trigger new insights into their own lives and feelings. For secondary school teachers, the course demonstrates the feasibility of intellectually demanding cultural themes which cut right across existing subject boundaries.

However, it has been argued that the MACOS conception of culture is selective; that it is symptomatic of the liberal, middle class intellectual ideology (Inglis 1974). For example, it does not provide children with cues to reflect on the political dimensions of culture. Exciting and absorbing though its ideas are, they seem curiously alien to the idioms of thought and expression of urban working class children. It may stimulate thought about culture, but will it stimulate cultural action?

Three years later (1968) Bruner commented wryly on what he had learnt from MACOS and its reception in schools. 'The experience has taught us not to be casual about means . . . What seems like a simple pedagogical premise would, if implemented, produce a minor revolution in teacher training or in film making or in school budgeting.'

For a much more detailed description and review of critiques of Man: A Course of Study, see Jenkins (1975) and Stenhouse (1975).

(3) Midwinter (1972) – Curriculum development and the social environment in 'educational priority areas'

The challenge facing Eric Midwinter was very different from that facing Bruner, for his task was to stimulate cultural action. It was to find ways of improving the educational life of socially deprived urban areas, defined by the Plowden Report as areas where educational handicaps are reinforced by social handicaps, such as large families, overcrowding, housing shortage and stress.

Midwinter seldom uses the term 'culture' as such, stressing more the idea of school-community collaboration and the need to capitalise on the immediate urban social environment. The three extracts that follow are, as before, very selective. The first and third extracts are from pp. 12-13 and p. 25 of *Social Environment and the Urban School*; the second is from *Projections*, p. 31. They are concerned with children of primary school age.

(1) THE URBAN CURRICULUM

The teacher's task should be to acquaint these children as profoundly as possible with the context in which they live. From this they might just reach out past a resigned acceptance of their lot, or a crude, negative reaction against it, to a clear articulation of their needs and to positive

11

responses to those needs. Eventually a community must save itself, and education could be one of the keys to the necessary self-awareness on which reconstruction might be built. We must not so much move from the known to the unknown, as to make the known more knowable.

. . . First, this is not . . . inward looking, designed to nurture a ghetto mentality . . . It is an attempt to open the eyes of urban children dynamically and critically to the locality as a secure base for educational advance. It means a curriculum more social and less academic than hitherto, but it need be no less creatively and intellectually exhilarating.

Second, a community orientated or environmentally based curriculum is more likely to engage the involvement of parents and other members of the community. If we believe in the need for a harmony of interest between school and home, and thus a stable balance of support for the child between school and home, then it is urgently necessary to harmonise the cultural content and values between them. . .

(2) SOCIAL ENVIRONMENTAL PROBES

Perhaps our social environment probes are the most straightforward examples with which to begin . . . Two of them examine with immense detail and care some immediate social agency such as the school itself, the church, the street, or the shops. This is in part a physical examination, searching out the minutiae of fabric ostensibly well known to the children and drawing on varied media to represent it. Another investigates the cultural and literary heritage of the area, looking critically, for example, at the differing religious sects and other institutions around about or recreating, verbally and dramatically, local life and stories. Another bases its local studies on features like street surfaces and furniture, derivation of street names and changes in building usage.

12

Creative expression is another *modus operandi*. The group in question choose a theme, such as 'occupations', 'streets', 'money', 'transport' or 'the city'. The children apply all creative media, verbal, oral, dramatic, artistic, in two and three dimensions, musical and dance, to representation of the theme, flexing their creative muscles on matters native to them, learning to conceive of responses to immediate issues.

(3) HOW TO OPERATE THE PROGRAMME

At least five sessions a week (say three afternoons and two mornings) should be spent on social environmental work. There should daily activities, e.g.

(1) Each child keeps a diary or pictorial scrapbook, in order to build his own autobiography.
(2) A class logbook or timechart is kept to trace the development or history of the class. There might be associated daily exercises on the weather, class plants and animals, children's heights and weights, etc.

A proposed week's work might be:

Monday Internal 'social' work, e.g. discussion of some school precept or rule such as punctuality, tidiness, monitors, cooking, care of pets, etc.

Tuesday and Wednesday Work on the current topic.

Thursday External or communal work, e.g. help for old age pensioners; landscaping or gardening in school playground; concert for hospital; writing to sick children or invalids, etc.

Friday Visit or be visited. Tours of locality or invitation to people to talk about jobs (preferably parents). Class parental activity of some kind.

By and large there is nothing new about any of this. It is the scale of it that is innovatory. Different schools and teachers will tackle the problem in differing degrees and with varying emphasis. The format is proposed as a stalking horse. The essential factor is the urgent, all-important character of the enterprise. . .

What comes through most clearly from the limited extracts given here is a sense of the will and practical know-how to combine idealism and realism. In comparison with the MACOS rationale the approach is crude; there is little concern with nuances of meaning, with discrimination of the different forms of thinking and methods of enquiry that are involved in understanding the cultural environment. In comparison with the Smith, Stanley and Shores rationale, the approach seems piecemeal; little space is given to the analysis of wider, longer-term problems of culture. It might be argued, in fact, that Midwinter over-emphasises the more tangible, surface features of culture and community. It could also be said that his case has the vigour to mobilise those who are already dissatisfied with urban curricula; but it does not have the intellectual panache and challenge (of Bruner's approach) to persuade thoughtful conservatives.

It is more to the point that Midwinter is trying to resolve a problem characterised by pressures, conflicts, and scarce resources of time, money, energy and professional expertise. The key resource must be people: community rapport and support, commitment to the idea of cultural regeneration, and capacities to capitalise on local culture, even in its pedestrian forms.

Summary
The three approaches to curriculum in terms of culture which were outlined confront different situations but have certain common characteristics. All try to see people's thought and action, especially teaching itself, within its total context: to recognise underlying environmental forces of

which people may be unaware; the symbols and ideas available; people's feelings, beliefs, values. All three approaches work through what seems a contradiction: although people's conceptions and expectations, not least teachers', are shaped by culture, yet people can and do shape culture.

Further reading
It is important to see all the main extracts quoted (Smith, Stanley and Shores (1957), Bruner (1966) and Midwinter (1972)) in context. If the first of these is unobtainable, Broudy, Smith and Burnett (1964) will serve almost as well. For two interpretations of how the basic idea of a common core curriculum might be applied in this country, see Lawton (1973 and 1975), and White (1973), though note that their interpretations of the idea diverge significantly from the original American conception. The issues raised are further discussed in chapter 10 of this book. For a much more detailed description and review of critiques of Man: A Course of Study, see Jenkins (1975) and Stenhouse (1975). To get a more detailed description of how children can become involved in the community and develop a sense of their ability to influence their *milieu*, see Rennie, Lunzer and Williams (1974).

2 CULTURE, PLANNING AND THE PRACTICAL

All three approaches to curriculum described in chapter 1 try to resolve a central practical dilemma: all entail programmes of change which seem to presuppose the very qualities and abilities that they are intended to foster, such as cultural sensibility, cooperativeness, social concern, etc. In this chapter we try to show how this problem can be seen within a particular conception of curriculum planning.

Several points about the teacher's cultural role have to be made first. Even where teachers unreflectively follow a syllabus or textbook, they still choose the emphasis in children's experiencing of that prescribed content. That emphasis will be influenced by teachers' consciousness of culture, or lack of it, and their values about it. Further, no teacher can 'transmit' culture effectively without interpreting and responding to the consciousness of his pupils; that is to say, without understanding *their* culture. Teachers also have to interpret and respond to the culture embodied in school organisation, in order to relate diverse short-term teaching decisions to school life as a whole. Through their pacing and coordination of children's classroom work within the wider school timetable, for instance, teachers sustain and impart our culture's inherited conceptions of how people should work together on complex long-term tasks. Hence teachers' day-to-day decisions provide cultural models to children of how limited resources of time, energy, money and other resources should be allocated in such tasks.

The overall point to be underlined about the teacher's role is this. Whether teachers recognise it or not, they do much more than transmit knowledge. They select from and mediate culture for children; and in so doing they make valuations of culture. To become conscious of the teacher's varied role as a mediator and valuer of culture is to begin to reinterpret assumptions about curriculum planning and teaching. Curriculum planning can be seen as a form of cultural enquiry. But we need a framework of ideas within which this conception can be discussed and given practical force.

To relate the three concepts, curriculum, experience and culture, is useful in two main ways. First, to see the curriculum as experience enables teachers to bring into focus the *activity* of experiencing, as distinct from the *content* of experience, the more familiar usage of the concept. For example, it maintains attention on the activities through which students learn to select from and shape the content of their incoming experience, as well as on the formal subject matter (or syllabus) that teachers hopefully transmit. Through a focus on the activity of experiencing we can think more sharply about the *quality* of experience. As we shall see in later chapters, however, we are not very good at talking about the process of experience in schools, partly because the words available are irretrievably ambiguous and time for curriculum discussion is usually short. Thus there are times when we have to talk of curriculum either as subject matter, knowledge to be 'transmitted', or as the practice of teachers.

Secondly, to see curriculum experience as a selection from culture enables teachers to think about what they may otherwise take for granted because it is so familiar: beliefs about which aspects of particular social groups' or generations' ways of experiencing and ordering life can or should be imparted to the coming generation. For example, as Smith,

17

Stanley and Shores imply, schools ought surely to think about the case for drawing upon forms and funds of experience which are well developed in society but excluded from school curricula. Skills in interpersonal relations and moral sensitivity, understanding of work culture and economic forces, political wisdom, are only three untapped reservoirs of experience of great significance in our wider culture. Are these potential cultural resources omitted from most curricula because they are too difficult for children? As we shall see in chapters 8 to 10, the answer is partly that the constraints under which teachers work and the way schools are organised make such changes difficult to visualise.

However, you may already have experienced the conflict inherent in curriculum thinking between abstract, theoretical considerations, in this case 'culture', and the concrete, practical demands of teaching itself. This conflict can be partly resolved through the adoption of a broader conception of the scope of curriculum planning. The way that people usually talk of planning suggests a limited process: devising a programme, blueprint or map to be followed. But in complex aspects of life, such as education, where sequences of action arise from other people's expectations, impinge on them, and influence other people's subsequent actions, this is too simple a view of planning. Curriculum planning is often more a matter of planning *with* people than planning *for* them. The crucial aspects of the *overall* planning process may not be the drafting of the plan itself. What matters most may be: (1) when and why a problem needing a plan is recognised, and what appraisals and assumptions enter into perceptions of the problem; (2) the generally implicit negotiation and interaction with other people, including children, who are affected by the plan; (3) the evaluations and adjustments that follow it.

It helps to think of this wider process of curriculum planning as society's means to an intelligent continuous adaptation to the demands of a changing cultural environment.

18

When teachers plan the curriculum on behalf of society, they project themselves and their values about culture and the quality of life. Hence, to plan intelligently, so the American philosopher John Dewey argued, is to do so self-consciously, critically – hypothesising, for example, about sources of cultural malaise, and possible solutions. Seen as hypotheses about cultural development, curriculum plans either 'work' or do not. If plans 'work', we develop new understanding based on clarity about what went well. If plans fail, then the thought given to them helps to identify where we erred; and enables us to rethink our assumptions.

Of course, it is not as simple as that. Value judgements and interpretations of complex practical situations are involved in all phases of curriculum planning. There is no formal testing of hypotheses, Nevertheless, Dewey's view of the potential role of planning in social life enables us to see how curriculum planning can be a process of cultural enquiry through action. In which case, curriculum 'theory' and 'practice' converge in reciprocal interplay: ideas modifying our perceptions of the practicalities of teaching; curriculum action and its outcomes modifying our use of ideas.

Yet we are still talking in general terms about judgements which depend on who makes them, when, and in what particular circumstances. But however specific they are to situations, particular decisions about teaching hinge on the decision-maker's view of the situation and the direction in which he thinks it ought to develop. His capacity to see the situation in context and to recognise what can and what cannot be changed are central. But this in turn depends on the ideas, the symbolic forms which he brings to bear to mediate the situation and focus on its hidden relationships.

Much has been written elsewhere on curriculum planning as a rational sequential process (for a concise and serviceable approach, see Lawton, 1973, chapter 1). Our concern is to articulate a way of thinking about planning which (1) recognises that people approach it with very different roles and responsibilities, and (2) links the resolution of short-term matters (what equipment is necessary *now,* which questions to set children *tomorrow*) to long-term issues (what ideals of culture people should come to have, how institutions should promote these ideals).

The diagram (Figure 2.1) below helps to illustrate the point. Like any curriculum model, it is a simplified, selective representation of experience; it filters out many relationships in curriculum and articulates others. But it serves to bring into relief aspects of curriculum construction which are otherwise taken for granted or not conceptualised. For example, the consciousness of a teacher directly affected by curriculum plans tends to focus mainly on matters which can be classified in the top middle box. In thinking about curriculum he rehearses in his mind what *he* will actually have to *do.* Though we may define the curriculum as what children *ought* to *experience,* the teacher's initial concern is to form a conception or image of what *content* he will have to teach, by

Focus of curriculum concern / Level and form of decision	What actually happens (the empirical)	What changes might be practicable (the prudential)	What ought to be (the prescriptive)
Lesson planning and pedagogic decision			
School and/or departmental planning			
National and/or L.E.A. curriculum policy			

2.1 *Curriculum Planning. Different Foci of Attention and Conceptions of Curriculum*

what *methods,* and what *activities will occupy children. His judge-ment about what would be practicable for him* depends on his com-paring this conception with (1) his knowledge of what nor-mally happens (how children respond in crowded class-rooms, etc.) and (2) his values and understanding about what ought to be the case (for example, subject matter *ought* to be logically sequential, and *ought* to be adapted to chil-dren's individual needs, etc.). In this sense, curriculum plan-ning can be seen as a matter more of the intuitive and immediate *matching of images* rather than of the logical and sequential weighing of propositions.

But this intuitive matching of images can become part of a rational, self-conscious process of curriculum planning: by seeing it first in the context of a longer *temporal* process, sec-ondly, in the context of a wider *social* process. In the case of the first, intuitive judgements can become components in rational planning by being seen as part of the situational approach to curriculum design described in chapter 9; or, in rare cases when planning starts with a clean slate, by being seen as part of the 'rational-deductive' approach described by Tyler (1949), Lawton (1973), etc. ('Rational-deductive' implies that means can be deduced from an initial statement of aims and objectives.) Intuitive judgement can also be seen over time as phases in a self-conscious process of curriculum deliberation, that is to say, of negotiation and practical judgement as described by Schwab (1970). As integral parts of the semi-formal process of curriculum deliberation, the views of other interested people act as stimuli, checks and modifiers of teachers' personal flow of ideas and images about what is possible and desirable in curriculum.

Self-conscious understanding of the second context of intuitive judgement, that of a wider social process, is equally important. The point is that when a teacher plans a par-ticular lesson or teaching strategy, his conception of what is possible is limited by decisions made elsewhere and guided by consideration of a wider organisational context (such as

21

the overall school timetable, availability of rooms, community and examinations requirements). When these decisions are made, the dominant factors may be less the pupils' learning experience than what is administratively and economically feasible; and how decisions affect teachers' status, responsibilities, free time, professional aspirations, etc. The larger the school, the more precarious is the state of social balance which these decisions may affect. The individual teacher's understanding of this state of balance may crucially influence the style and direction of his lesson planning and the particular cultural emphases in his teaching. When we talk about 'curriculum' in this context, we are referring mainly to complex webs of professional and organisational practice.

Let us return to the diagram. Whatever level and form of curriculum decision making we are concerned with at a particular time (very few teachers are restricted solely to the top row of concerns), we have to match the ideal with the actual *as they affect that social context*. But this is not to say that we are imprisoned by the circumstances of that context, for example, by the desire of headteachers to avoid upsetting a complex timetable. If we understand the interdependence between the different contexts of decision making, then there is always scope for modification of constraints. Some organisational constraints are so complex (for example those which structure choice of subjects in large comprehensive schools) that they can only be changed by lengthy negotiation over a long period of time. Others hinge on the cultural assumptions of decision makers, assumptions which can be reinterpreted where there are good, professional relationships between staff, and between school and community. Examples might be: assumptions about the relative priority of teaching aims, such as memorisation in relation to skill-acquisition; assumptions about the role of tests and examinations, whether they are primarily to diagnose learning difficulties, to provide incentives, to rank children's abilities,

22

etc.

The point to be emphasised here is that by looking more analytically at the relationship between classroom constraints, how decisions are made outside the classroom, and how such decisions accumulate to influence cultural conceptions and expectations, we develop new perceptions of what is possible. Through consciousness of this interdependence we can nurture longer-term plans or cultural projects while still meeting the unremitting demands of day-to-day teaching. In doing so, the crucial decisions may be those made at the central or school level of planning shown in Figure 2.1.

The devising of 'mental maps' (such as Figure 2.2) of the interlocking facets and levels of curriculum decisions may help us here. Figure 2.2 was devised from the point of view of a national curriculum project. Although an individual teacher seldom has to appraise the curriculum 'system' in such terms, it can help him to see particular trends in perspective; and to support or oppose them more reflectively. It is an aid to curriulum (or cultural) navigation, as opposed to cultural drift.

These analyses help to crystallise what we think *with* in the overall planning process, rather than what we think *about*. But if the idea of curriculum development as cultural development is to be made practical, we have to recognise the complexity of the existing curriculum decision making system in England and many other countries, and how it limits what schools see as feasible. It is a historically rooted, cumulative response to past perceptions of problems. They were and still are problems of reconciling different interests and unevenly distributed resources of professional talent, time, money, etc., in which rather conservative views of education have only very gradually been reinterpreted. (See Lawton 1973, chapters 5 and 6, for a concise review of socio-historical factors.)

Partly because of its piecemeal evolution, the decision

Changes of ideas lead to modifications in teachers' perceptions of geography and of their roles in its teaching, and hence in dominant styles of school geography. The same teacher may well express something of each style within a day's work, for good teaching has elements of both traditional and 'new' approaches. But even though the

Cultural change through evolving ideas and technology

Assumptions about the nature of geography and the role of the geographer	Aims in school geography and related form of assessment
STYLE I Pattern recognition from maps 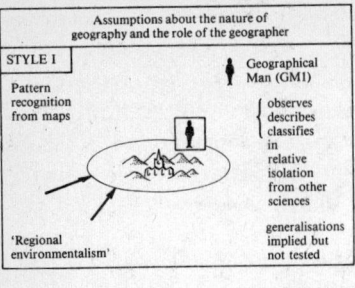 Geographical Man (GM1) observes / describes / classifies / in relative isolation from other sciences 'Regional environmentalism' — generalisations implied but not tested	1. Factual knowledge of 'world stage'; man-land relationships in regions; basic map and graphic skills 2. Contributions of geography to world citizenship stressed 3. Common questions test recall and map interpretation
STYLE II New techniques enable more penetrative pattern recognition 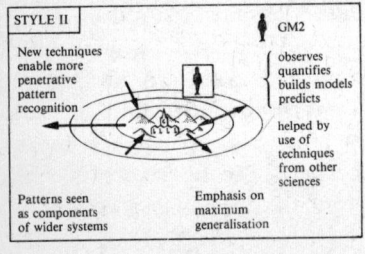 GM2 observes / quantifies / builds models / predicts helped by use of techniques from other sciences Patterns seen as components of wider systems — Emphasis on maximum generalisation	1. Concept acquisition; interpretation of data, application of principles, hypothesis testing 2. Contribution of geography to scientific thinking stressed 3. New assessment techniques enable more intellectually searching and objective questions testing common performances
STYLE III 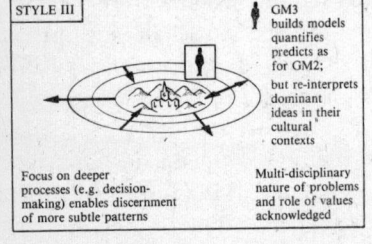 GM3 builds models / quantifies / predicts as for GM2; but re-interprets dominant ideas in their cultural contexts Focus on deeper processes (e.g. decision-making) enables discernment of more subtle patterns — Multi-disciplinary nature of problems and role of values acknowledged	1. Concepts and skills in geography are related to other areas of experience, practical problems and clarification of values. 2. Contribution to student's wider sensibility stressed 3. Scope for individual studies and open-ended questions; course work provides more feedback

KEY GM 'Geographical Man' MG 'Man in Geography'
'Geographical Man' (the geographer) has to make assumptions about the people (Man in Geography) the results of whose actions (e.g. land use) he studies. As GM's technology and values change, so may the characteristics which he attributes to people (MG) making decisions which modify the spatial environment.

2.2 *Styles of school geography*

model of 'dominant styles' in school geography simplifies a complex reality, it enables a sharper analysis to be made of underlying assumptions and relationships. Thus it helps to explain why change is generally slow and piecemeal.

Teaching-learning relationships	Planning and management of curriculum change
Transmission-reception model 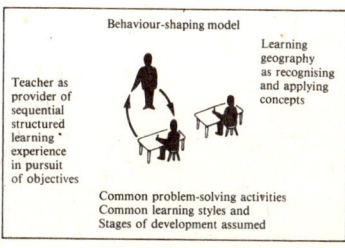 The teacher as expositor with use of visual aids sample studies etc. Learning geography as accumulating facts and practising skills	Programmes of subject-matter to be covered; change initiated through externally determined syllabuses New textbooks necessary
Behaviour-shaping model Learning geography as recognising and applying concepts Teacher as provider of sequential structured learning experience in pursuit of objectives Common problem-solving activities Common learning styles and Stages of development assumed	Programmes of concepts and skills to be acquired and objectives to be achieved Objectives are externally decided; computerisation tends to encourage standardisation and centralisation Curriculum 'packages' necessary

Interactionist model
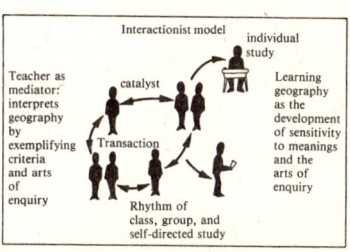
individual study
Teacher as mediator: interprets geography by exemplifying criteria and arts of enquiry
catalyst
Transaction
Learning geography as the development of sensitivity to meanings and the arts of enquiry
 	
Rhythm of class, group, and self-directed study
	Criteria for selection of subject-matter and learning experience
	
	New consultative processes and co-ordinating roles evolved, to reconcile flexibility, continuity and comparability in
	  (a) curriculum
	  (b) assessment
	
	Diversity of resources and facilities necessary

GM1   depends mainly on maps and intuitive recognition to discern relationships.
GM2   helped by statistical techniques and computers discerns otherwise hidden aggregative patterns.
GM3   helped by growing understanding of deeper processes, looks for new forms of data and patterns.
MG1   It is assumed that his actions on the environment are in direct response to physical factors.
MG2   It is assumed that his actions on the environment are filtered by economic considerations of least effort, least cost, etc.
MG3   It is assumed that rational actions on the environment take different forms related to ideology, myth, and social organisation.

making system presents individual teachers with little support and incentive to see their work in cultural terms. Because it has worked passably well, the system has inbuilt inertia; or, if you prefer, stability and resilience. Hence, the last section of the book, chapters 9 and 10, proposes new strategies of curriculum decision making which reflect: (1) the central role of the school in mediating the environing culture, subject to the procedural values of practical experimentation, openness to criticism and reinterpretation of ideas; (2) basic selections for our cultural experience to be drawn on by all schools in order to foster shared values.

We said that curriculum 'theory' and practice can be brought into interplay through a broad conception of curriculum planning as cultural enquiry and action; but you may still feel uneasy at the distance between the abstract idea of culture and the difficult tasks for teachers that school-based curriculum development suggests. Why is most current thinking and writing about curriculum concerned with a more limited level of theory, with a narrower view of the task of development? For example, in England and Wales most Schools Council projects have either used no explicit theoretical framework at all or have concerned themselves with detailed analyses of objectives and programmes of teaching within circumscribed areas of the curriculum. It has to be accepted that there are two major difficulties in the use of an overall (or 'holistic') framework of ideas for curriculum development.

The first major difficulty is that of the very scope of the concept of culture. The classic definition of culture comes from nineteenth century anthropology. It is 'that complex whole which includes knowledge, belief, art, morals, law, custom and other capabilities acquired by man as a member of society' (Tylor 1871), but even twenty years ago two eminent anthropologists had identified 164 alternative definitions of the concept (Kroeber and Kluckhohn 1952). Not surprisingly both radical and conservative teachers invoke culture, arguing that education cannot help but be influenced by culture. They do not agree about how teachers should be conserving culture or reappraising it, but their use of the concept is similarly diffuse. You may already have sensed the central problem of culture and curriculum. To grasp the interrelation of factors in curriculum, we need a more general idea. The concept of culture can be applied to almost any curriculum view or experience; but can we actually use it to guide what we do? It is what some philosophers criticise as a portmanteau or rubber-bag word. You can get what you want into it. Because it seems to describe so much, it may describe very little. To get practical insights into curriculum we have to develop clear ways of talking about culture which really help to illuminate what shapes experience, and which influences its educative quality. This we aim to do in chapters 3 to 8.

The second major difficulty in the use of an overall perspective on curriculum development is this. What exactly is it for? How should it te used? It should be emphasised that its main function is to guide action itself and to enhance the interpretation of first-hand experience of curriculum actualities. It does so by enabling us to coordinate our value judgements and appraisals of situations in many different contexts over lengthy periods of time. It helps us to detach ourselves from otherwise personalised curriculum dilemmas by seeing them as aspects of more general cultural experience. We can then reconceptualise and redefine curriculum tasks more coolly and adroitly. But an overall framework can also serve as an ideology in inducing the commitment and mood to face practicalities and to work with other people upon what are inevitably often untidy and frustrating cultural projects. Furthermore, such a framework is of practical value to teachers and others responsible for curriculum decisions in the schools.

The main function of an overall theory of curriculum development as cultural development is *not* to explain what teachers do or children learn, in the sense that formal scientific theory explains the occurrence of phenomena by showing how they are covered by natural 'laws'. *Nor* is its main function to indicate what must be done to achieve a given end, as in applied science and technology (see Hirst 1966 and Moore 1974 for a fuller discussion of this). Of course, it should be in accord with empirical theories, for example in psychology and sociology, and with technical advice about pedagogy itself. The more links with these to which an overall valuative and interpretative framework points, the more useful it will be. But it is misleading to attribute the traditional lack of interest in England with broader ideas about culture to their not being more 'practical' in the empirical and technical sense. That is not primarily what they are for. This lack of interest in more general ideas is probably more a reflection of healthy scepticism about their misuse. Too often theory building and curriculum planning become introspective and self-indulgent, insulated from practical experimentation and criticism. So long as curriculum analysis is a dominantly armchair activity, it is possible to filter out and ignore inconvenient facts (about organisational complexities, and teachers' and pupils' interests, for instance) by interposing a preconceived framework of ideas or theory. The framework which we have sketched is intended to avoid this self-deception by recognising facts about school organisation, parents' attitudes, etc., as aspects of culture. As such, their discernment and reinterpretation are integral parts of thoughtful curriculum planning.

In the last chapter we mentioned how Jerome Bruner had come to reinterpret his earlier and penetrating conception of culture and teaching. His views about the requirements that overall theory should meet provide an appropriate conclusion to this chapter:

A theory fares well when it accords with a culture's conception of its function. Each culture has conceptions of the nature of a child, some conceptions of what constitutes

28

good adults. It also has, at some implicit level, some conception of what it regards as the appropriate *means* of getting from the nature of the child to the nature of the adult. If a pedagogical theorist is to move that culture, he must forge a theory that relates to that range of acceptable means. . . [The educator who] formulates theory without regard to the political, economic and social setting of the educational process courts triviality and merits being ignored in the community and the classroom. (Bruner, 1968)

Summary

In curriculum thinking we have to alternate between two modes of experience: on the one hand, the analysis of curriculum constraints, such as lack of resources, parental and teacher attitudes, the unintended effects of change in complex organisation, and so on; on the other hand, the articulation and review of ideas, beliefs and values about the directions in which children's learning experience and curriculum organisation ought to develop. The distinctive arts of curriculum lie in the matching and recurrent rematching of the two within an overall conception of planning and culture.

Further reading
Tyler (1949) provides the classic approach to curriculum planning in a lucid readable form, which Lawton (1973) has adapted and updated to take account of current thinking in this country. Richardson (1975) is invaluable in illustrating the need to see planning within schools within a wider, superficially less 'rational' set of social relations. She shows that issues of teachers' roles, responsibilitites and status, and the boundaries that they draw in their work are more potent influences than is usually acknowledged.

3 CULTURE AND SOCIAL PROCESS

In the previous chapters we recognised that culture is an elusive idea, that it is a process rather than a thing. We can regard it as the field of interaction between (1) men's social relationships and conventions, (2) the symbolic forms available to them for focusing on and coordinating experience, and (3) their systems of belief, values and action. In the next four chapters we shall consider in turn how each of these elements bears on the curriculum. In this chapter we concentrate on the first of them – culture seen as social process.

Two points should be stressed. Though it is a short chapter (because there is accessible literature elsewhere dealing with the main ideas), it is one of the most important. Secondly, sociology uses a variety of perspectives and concepts whose appropriateness to different educational problems is controversial. Our concern is the usefulness of these concepts in practical curriculum judgement. To get us under way, we shall generalise about their usefulness in a way that will stick in the gullets of many sociologists, though many will agree with the position towards which we argue. For our purposes, we shall distinguish three broad sociological approaches: those in terms primarily of *social function; social conflict and symbolic interaction;* and the *sociology of knowledge.* When used selectively and sceptically, each enhances common sense views of curriculum.

Sociologists find it hard to establish causal links between social processes at the different levels of generality and decision-making noted in chapter 2 (Figure 2.1). For example, it is difficult to use the same concepts in talking about: (1) social processes at the macro-social or societal level (such as changes in national occupational structure, and hence long-term demands for particular curriculum skills and qualities); (2) social processes at a middle level (for example, those within a bounded community or institution, such as the effect on a selective school of becoming an all-ability, comprehensive school); and (3) social processes at a micro- or group level (for example, the effect of classroom milieu on teacher-pupil relations and patterns of questioning). However, although a sociologist may rightly decide to concentrate his research at a particular level of generality, the teacher, in his role as curriculum builder, has to make overall practical judgements about how these levels do or should interrelate. Let us make the tentative assumption that for the teacher the appropriateness of the sociological perspectives to be discussed depends on which level of process is his immediate concern.

Broad social forces and the 'functionalist' perspective
The most basic questions in curriculum are whether schools should simply respond to the expectations and demands of society, should progressively adapt to changes in society, or should seek to influence the direction of change. For example, technological change is modifying the significance of child-bearing and rearing in nearly all women's lives. Most women now finish bringing up their children by the age of forty and have more than thirty years of active life ahead of them. But current culture provides few forms of expression for their feelings or outlets for the abilities after child-rearing. Serious discussion of the underlying values and social issues is restricted to a small, highly educated minority. The prob-

lems are felt and sensed, but remain undefined, rather than brought into consciousness. Are they too complex for schools to take into account in their curriculum planning?

In understanding the nature of the task, the first step is recognition that the cultural environment is much more complex than any mechanistic system, and that the changes within it ensue from 'messages' and flows of information rather than physical forces. Hence the sociologist acknowledges the importance of 'ideas', symbolic forms and forms of expression which schools promote, but stresses their social *function*. For example, shared ideas and skills get things done efficiently and raise our standard of living (what the sociologist calls the *instrumental* function of culture). Secondly, they sustain and regulate people's ideals and values, hence sustaining the cohesion of social groups (the *normative* function of culture). Thirdly, they enable people to express and share their emotions, and hence to come to terms with their feelings and to celebrate life collectively (the *expressive* function of culture). Jokes, ritualised grumbles, ceremonies, uniforms, emblems, etc., for example, have a key normative and expressive function as symbols in school culture.

This perspective may dispose us to take a fairly cautious view about how the curriculum ought to respond to social change. For example, T. S. Eliot was implicitly emphasising the normative and expressive functions of culture when he observed that culture is what makes life worth living. Because he thought that in an industrialised society schools inevitably concentrated on instrumental aspects of culture (basic skills in literacy, mathematics) or surface aspects of high culture, he took a pessimistic view of the effect of mass education. He believed that schooling devitalised popular culture because teachers inevitably disparaged its symbolic forms, its traditions, myth, dialect, folk wisdom and moral precepts, etc., and deprived them of their expressive and cohesive force (Eliot 1948; see also Bantock 1970).

Eliot was such a bold and original thinker that he went on

to suggest that class divisions in society served to sustain and enrich culture. He argued, for example, that society needs a leisured upper class, sheltered from instrumental demands, to develop high culture. Only a minority of the population can be initiated into its sensibilities and only gradually at that. But the idea of the social function of culture can be put to more radical use when the relationship with social *structure* is more closely examined. The metaphor 'structure' focuses our attention on the relatively stable skeleton of social life, the shared conventions about class and status, roles and mutual obligations, opportunities for and restrictions on access to knowledge, wealth and power.

It can be argued, for example, that the structuring of subjects in the curriculum, together with the way we select which children should study which subjects, reflects middle class control over the way in which adolescents are allocated to their positions in society. It can be said, for example, that the function of examinations which test pupils' abilities in the intellectualised operations of academic subjects is to maintain the present class structure of society. It is claimed that examinations and the opportunity to ascend the social ladder are open to all; but in practice, so the argument runs, the culture and facilities of middle class homes in Britain enable middle class children to adopt and respond more 'successfully' than working class children to the stylised way in which 'subjects' are taught (for further discussion of these complex and controversial issues see, for example, Banks 1968 and Hopper in Brown 1973).

Awareness of social structure can make us more aware that the selection and organisation of subjects and pupil-teacher relationships are not as disinterested, as 'purely educational', as they seem. Yet it is surely an exaggeration to suppose that curriculum decisions do nothing more than serve the (class biased) functions of society. Arguably, when mass education was first set up in industrialised societies, it did little more than meet the needs of those societies, or rather of their ruling classes, for a literate, socially disciplined labour force. But since then the teaching profession has become much better educated, socially conscious and disposed to nurture its own interests rather than only reflect those of society.

Over time, moreover, individual schools develop their own culture. What we often describe as the 'climate' or 'ethos' of a school is really the outcome of its normative and expressive order built up by successive intakes of individuals, interacting with one another under the influence of expectations already established (see Shipman 1968 for a lucid account of the sociology of the school). These expectations can be said to constitute a 'hidden curriculum', which transmits tacit cultural messages. It has been suggested, for example, that the three central 'messages' of most infant schools are that the child must learn to live (1) in a crowd, (2) under constant evaluation, and (3) under conditions of power (Jackson 1968). But the cultural 'messages' of schools are almost certainly more complex and variable than we yet understand. For instance, a recent study (Nash 1973) suggested that the constant evaluation with which children have to learn to cope comes as much from each other as from the teacher. It is not a simple case of the teacher imparting cultural expectations to children who are free of them. There are many social factors interacting in classrooms, and interacting differently in different classrooms; and much more empirical research is needed before we can speak confidently about the forces operating within classroom culture.

Micro-processes in classrooms and staffrooms: interactionist perspectives

But research into the imparting of cultural messages, into the dynamics and form of 'cultural reproduction', is not at all easy. Imagine sitting in a variety of classrooms over several months, trying to decide what exactly, amongst all the other

34

'messages' and happenings, counted as basic cultural messages. Equally to the point, consider how you would convince a range of sceptical people, such as teachers, that your findings were either useful or true. If the researcher starts with the assumption that the school's cultural messages will reflect society's class and occupational structure, that they will serve its political and economic needs, this may lead him to ignore or fail to notice happenings that do not fit this picture of the curriculum system. To give a very brief example: the effects of inflexible examinations in schools and colleges are sometimes attributed to the influence of a competitive economic system, obliging teachers and students to concentrate only on what is examined. But examination boards often argue that the pressure towards traditional examinations comes mainly from teachers themselves; that it is they (the teachers) who exalt examination results, perhaps because they need tangible measures of success; and that particular forms of examination papers are shaped by competing interests amongst teachers.

Hence an alternative sociological approach to the curriculum focuses on social conflict, and especially upon the role of symbolic forms and ritual in transforming and reconciling the inevitably varied and discordant aspirations of teachers, children, parents, employers. Instead of glossing over such tensions by appealing to some common social function, the approach brings them into relief. It shows, for example, that there are many opposing views about the curriculum held by teachers of the same subject; and that the curriculum is given only a superficial cohesion and unity of purpose by the power and authority of senior decision-making bodies, such as examination committees, or persons, such as school principals.

It follows that to understand how curriculum patterns emerge we should perhaps look less at social systems and structures than at particular situations or episodes in which curriculum power is taken, given, challenged or negotiated

(Shaw 1975). This can be seen not only in staff meetings when curriculum policies are discussed, or perhaps enunciated and passively accepted, but also in classrooms where the teacher establishes or fails to establish authority with the children. By the passivity, intransigence or rebelliousness of their response, children may greatly modify a teacher's original curriculum plans.

Emphasis shifts to the way in which teachers and children negotiate and thus create their own social realities, as distinct from subconsciously adapting to invisible but powerful social structures. There is not space to develop this approach here. It is variously termed the symbolic interactionist or phenomenological perspective and is well described by Berger and Luckmann (1967), Hargreaves (1973), Keddie (1971) and Musgrave (1973). It is akin to, though not identical with the approach described in chapters 4 and 5 of this book. The practical problem which it does not seem to resolve is this: what limits how far teachers and children can create their own cultural realities? Are there certain curriculum 'structures' which schools must acknowledge, and certain inescapable social conventions which they must honour?

Organisation, control and the sociology of knowledge
In recent years 'new directions' have been claimed for the sociology of education. The claim partly grew out of dissatisfaction with the crudeness of the functional approach when applied to life in schools and classrooms (Davies in Young 1971) and the seeming impossibility of deriving coherent theories or testable statements from conflict and symbolic interactionist approaches. But the main positive stimuli to develop a different stance came from two theorists, Pierre Bourdieu (1971) and Basil Bernstein (1971). Both were concerned with the distinctive characteristic of 'cultural reproduction' – the fact that although there are striking

differences between what happens in different schools and classrooms, yet there are undeniable similarities in the forms of experiencing that all schools provide in similar education systems. Both seek to explain these similarities in ways which do justice to what is intrinsic to the knowledge-getting and knowledge-transmitting processes, rather than to see schools and universities as mirrors of wider social and economic forces.

Bourdieu relates the similarities in the experience which schools provide to prevailing national intellectual styles at different phases of history, such as the tacit emphasis in both French schools and intellectual life upon formal reasoning and the habit of thinking of man in abstract, general terms. He argues that schools do much more than *reflect* these styles of thought:

> The school does not merely provide reference marks: it also maps out itineraries . . . programmes of thought. The intellectual and linguistic master-patterns organise a marked out area covered with compulsory turnings and one-way streets, avenues and blind alleys; within this area, thought can unfurl with the impression of freedom and improvisation because the marked out itineraries . . . are the very ones that it has covered many a time . . . (Bourdieu 1971, p. 196)

Bernstein's approach hinges on the insight that to facilitate knowledge-getting and knowledge-transmitting we have to classify experience, drawing boundaries between what counts as history, art, science, practical matters, ordinary life, etc. Otherwise we could transmit no clear cultural messages. But the act of classification is an act of social control. For example, secondary schools have traditionally accepted a clear cut division of teachers' work into 'subjects', within which teachers develop professional interests and senses of identity. To organise the curriculum in terms of themes or problems, which link different subjects, is therefore to do much more than change the timetable. It is to affect the way in which teachers and children classify the world and regulate their social relations. Integrated studies, for example, may bring changes in the status of subject teachers; they compel collaborative curriculum planning in schools, and thus prompt either more staff conflict or cohesion. Such changes inevitably modify the culture of the school.

Bernstein theorises that the way the cultural 'messages' of the school are classified and organised, the way that they are transmitted through teaching methods and teacher-pupil relations, and the way that they are evaluated, constitute an educational or cultural 'code'. This alarmingly abstract notion becomes clearer when we summarise the change in educational code which Bernstein suggests is taking place. It is suggested that the trend in curriculum development is from 'closed' curricula (collection codes) with strong boundaries and strong social control to 'open' curricula (integrated codes) with weak boundaries and weak social control.

Dimension	from (Collection codes)	to (Integrated codes)
Curriculum content	Separate subjects	Interdisciplinary
Pedagogy	Instruction	Enquiry activities
Organisation of teaching/learning	Rigid timetabling	Flexible timetabling
Pupil grouping	Homogeneous	Heterogeneous
Pupil choice	Limited	Extensive
Assessment	Single mode	Multiple modes
Basis of pupil control	Position in hierarchy	Personal relations
Teacher roles	Independent	Interdependent

(adapted from an unpublished paper by Eric Hoyle)

To take social theorising as far as this is really to return to the functional perspective which we criticised earlier. It is to assume that all these facets of curriculum *must* be linked,

38

which could be misleading, especially in the absence of extensive empirical studies to support it. Nevertheless the diagram has value in sensitising us to possible trends and to the *possible* interdependence of elements in the curriculum. Like all curriculum models, the diagram is for using, not for believing. Social theories are good servants but poor masters.

But to read Bourdieu and Bernstein is to meet another reason for interpreting their ideas carefully. The tortuous-ness of their prose and the unrelenting abstraction of their argument exhibits a wide gap between their styles of thought and the styles of thought of those people whose cultural world is the subject of their theorising. Can they really understand the consciousness of teachers yet write in a way that the majority of teachers find so alien? This is a criticism which slides too easily into anti-intellectualism; our point is the need to distinguish the different purposes of social theories about human consciousness and curriculum cul-ture. Such theories may be: (1) 'positivist' theories, modelled on those of the physical sciences, assuming that social or cur-riculum phenomena have constant meanings and can be pre-dicted and controlled; (2) interpretative theories, such as symbolic interactionism, in which the aim is simply to under-stand what is going on; (3) 'critical' theories, in which the aim is to enable people not only to understand their situation but to understand its underlying social structures and power relationships so as to influence them. This analysis belongs to the third category. We might, however, note in passing that it is not clear in which category Bourdieu's and Berns-tein's ideas might be placed. Perhaps they are best regarded as speculative theories whose main purpose is to stimulate thought and generate empirical research.

Summary
For the teacher in his role as curriculum maker what matters about sociological theories and concepts is how he uses them.

If he is alert to the different levels of generality at which they may apply and to their different purposes in thought, he can use them tentatively, as constructs, without ignoring or debunking the way in which teachers and parents think in their ordinary life. Perhaps the best criterion of the appropriateness of our use of sociological approaches is how we think about curriculum itself. Many teachers, the majority perhaps, accept the curriculum uncritically as a 'given', a fact of life, like the weather, unaffected by our consciousness. Alternatively, the curriculum may be regarded as created by individual teachers, negotiated, or forged out of social conflict. In this chapter we hope we have clarified why both these positions are too simple. There are social structures and functions in school life which teachers cannot ignore, and there are hidden processes and connections in the imparting of cultural messages which Bourdieu and Bernstein illuminate. The most honest way of regarding the curriculum is to see it partly as the outcome of the plans, aspirations, ideas and feelings of individual teachers and pupils, partly as the outcome of social processes with hidden patterns about which we can learn much more.

Further reading

Musgrave (1973) provides a concise review of the sociology of knowledge in relation to the curriculum, though it is important also to try to come to terms with Bourdieu (1971) and Bernstein (1971). Davies's paper (1971) in the same book of readings also repays the effort of careful reading. Hargreaves (1973) is very illuminating on classroom processes and a much more readable book. For a useful analysis of the relation between social theory and planning in general, see Bailey (1975).

4 SYMBOLIC FORMS AND SHARED EXPERIENCE

In the practical business of thinking about curriculum we continually need to use broad concepts, such as culture, to give us an overall or synoptic view of situations – especially the conflict situations, which as we noted in chapter 3, are inevitable in cultural change. Curriculum thinking hinges on the making of judgements. Good judgement entails alternation between the seeing of problems as a whole, which requires simplification, and the discerning of different aspects of problems, which requires analysis. In the former case the idea of culture provides a perspective for recognising the nature of a problem; for example, so that we initially conceive the planning of a lesson in terms of our mediating a chosen area of experience for children. But in the latter case, the sharper analysis of a problem, we need to focus on the different elements that enter into culture; for example, in order to mediate culture for children we need to understand how it helps to think of subject matter as culture. To think about it as a part of the 'complex whole which includes beliefs, values', etc., seems too blunt a tool for analysis.

Significantly, people seldom talk about culture in their everyday lives. Most people find themselves thinking about culture only when they have to bring back into consciousness aspects of thought, feeling and action that get taken for granted. These are generally those aspects which are so embedded in language, values, customs, etc., that they can only be acquired gradually, tacitly and often unquestioningly in community with others. The significant question to ask is: what are the situations in which we need to become conscious of culture as 'culture'?

Let us take the very problem of communication about curriculum as itself a telling example of a cultural problem. Why do existing ways of talking about schooling apparently need modification? In short, a curriculum problem can be described as a cultural problem when it is bound up with the adequacy of the ways in which people articulate and share experience and values which bear on the selection and structuring of experience in schools. Yet it is more than a problem of communication. The point is this. Culture develops as people evolve common basic ways of expressing and sharing experience through their use of symbols, language primarily, with reciprocal meanings. If there are discrepancies between what symbols mean to people, if they do not lead people to act in similar ways, or if the symbols do not seem to match the complex reality (such as curriculum), then we have a sense of cultural malaise. Feeling, thought and action are out of phase.

To understand the complex area of shared and individual experience that we label 'curriculum' we need to ask why it is difficult to talk about it in ways that seem businesslike, down to earth, but do not hide differences of meaning. Listen to a meeting of teachers discussing 'discovery learning'. Though they are apparently using the same concept, they are often referring to different things. When they actually use 'discovery learning' approaches, they concentrate on different aspects of the classroom situation. What children experience varies accordingly. Some experience discovery learning as play, others as worksheets, others as guided experiments. Books on curriculum are often based on definitions of terms like 'objectives', 'evaluation', 'strategy'. But actual curriculum situations are always more complex and fluid.

42

Listen to a group of teachers discussing assessment and their own pupils' achievement. At first they may seem to have accepted neutral definitions; for example, to regard assessment as the ranking of performances against particular criteria. But it is usually soon evident that this conception is too narrow to accommodate the experience and the wider meanings of 'assessment' involved.

In what situations do we find that things cannot be taken for granted, that there are problems of meaning and significance? There are those situations in which we have to make sense of an experience (What is that thing for? Is it a natural or cultural object? What do those gestures mean? What am I expected to do here?). There are situations in which a sense of unease, a felt anomaly in experience, or disagreement with others, prompts us to reappraise usages, conventions, beliefs, etc., that we had thought were stable, shared and readily understandable (What effect will that idea have on people's lives? Are we talking about the same problem? Is that really art/science/religion, etc.? Have they changed the rules?). And there are those situations in which we have to impart new ideas, values, expertise, to others in such a way that they will really understand them (What seems most basic? What cues must they be able to discern? How should we talk about it? At what should their feelings about it be directed?).

The first major point to note is that in each situation the idea of culture can be put to work to concentrate attention on forgotten or hidden connections between the basic ideas available and shared conventions between people through which the ideas acquire mutual significance. To see these problematic situations under the concept of culture is to retrieve or infer the processes in experience which have shaped what is significant in the situations for people. Because these processes can only develop over time through interaction with others, in ways that focus our attention on similar aspects of experience, they can be summed up and crystallised through a metaphor, that of culture. Its root

43

(non-metaphorical) meaning is nurture, the tending of organic growth.

The second major point is this. People most typically *initially* draw upon the idea of culture in puzzling or ambiguous contexts so that they can concentrate their attention on the tacit, gradual interplay of people's experience and forms of expression and symbols. But they tend subsequently to let their attention shift from these relationships to the more concrete, easily recognisable faces of the culturing process; for example, to etiquette or to dialect rather than to formulative conventions of human association and discourse. Or they may attend more to people's patterns of consumption, or to their answers to opinion polls, rather than to the structure of meaning in their day-to-day exchange with those people whose values they heed, and to their guiding images of the good life. In short, the way that we talk about culture may displace what originally aroused our attention, the need to recognise the ground-rules which steer people's thoughts, actions and feelings.

It is natural to concentrate on the concrete connotations of words but it may impoverish our consciousness. For example, some philosophers and linguists have argued that 'the structure of our language is relentless in forcing upon us "thing" conceptions. In English, we can transform any process or relationship into a "thing" by the simple expedient of naming "it" into a noun. We have done this with "rain" and "explosion", "thought" and "life" . . . [Language] has tended to favour the "fixed categories" people as against "the process and relationship" people' (Postman and Weingartner 1969). We shall use the idea of culture *as process* to focus on the quality of children's learning experience. It depends on the process by which teachers and parents select and foster their use of symbolic forms. We have no ready consciousness of how the forms shape our experience because they are what we think and feel with.

The sharing of feeling and thought, and hence the passing

on of inherited collective experience, can come about only through the use of common symbols and modes of expression. Words and other symbols, such as numbers, musical notation, diagrams, maps, etc., are the obvious examples; and, arguably, the most important. They are crucial in the culturing process because they mediate the content of experience. That is to say, they determine both what perceptual cues we attend to, how we select and group 'raw' or primary experience, and how we interpret it. Thus it is helpful to think of symbolic forms as 'filtering out' complex, confusing aspects of experience, and of 'amplifying' other aspects, hence making it easier to discern recurrent patterns in different situations. (Note that the idea of 'filters' and 'amplifiers' of experience is less deterministic than Bernstein's sociological concept of 'codes' or Bourdieu's 'master patterns' discussed in chapter 3, but the idea of the mediation and transformation of experience is common to both approaches.)

In effect, we do not experience the world directly. 'Physical reality seems to recede in proportion as man's symbolic activity advances. Instead of dealing with the things themselves, man is in a sense constantly conversing with himself. He has so enveloped himself in linguistic forms, artistic images, mythical symbols, or religious rites that he cannot see or know anything except by the interposition of this artificial medium' (Cassirer 1944).

One of the most suggestive accounts of the power of symbolic forms to mediate and transform experience was provided by Mrs Sullivan, the teacher of Helen Keller as a blind, deaf-mute child. She described the first occasion on which the child began to understand the function of language.

. . . This morning while she was washing, she wanted to know the name for 'water' . . . I spelled 'w-a-t-e-r' and thought no more about it until after breakfast. . . [Later on] we went out to the pump house, and I made Helen hold her mug under the spout while I pumped. As the cold water gushed forth, filling the mug, I spelled 'w-a-t-e-r' in Helen's free hand. The word coming so close upon the sensation of cold water rushing over her hand seemed to startle her. She dropped the mug and stood as one transfixed. A new light came into her face. The next morning she got up like a radiant fairy. She has flitted from object to object, asking the name of everything and kissing me for very gladness . . . She drops the signs and pantomime she used before, as soon as she has words to supply their place, and the acquirement of a new word affords her the liveliest pleasure. And we notice that her face grows more expressive each day. (Keller 1902, in Cassirer)

This is a telling illustration of a particular culturing process, but culturing processes take very varied and often more complex forms. To understand culture we have to be aware of how its formulative processes are differentiated into a wide range of symbolic and expressive forms. They range from: (1) crude pointers to experience, such as gestures; to (2) graphic simplification of experience, through direct visual representation or icons; to (3) evocative, often ambivalent ways of articulating and celebrating feelings, via images in art and religion, myth, ritual and jokes; to (4) the intricate structures of abstract symbols, detached from experience, in the form of mathematical formulae and scientific theories. The differing forms all select from and amplify experience, channelling our consciousness to some groupings and sequences of experience rather than others.

Summary
The following attempt to summarise the significance of symbolic forms provides a tentative conceptual 'map':

Observing is a function of the symbol systems the observer

46

has available to him. The more limited the symbol systems, in number and kind, the less one is able to 'see'.

A symbol system is, in effect, a point of view. The more ways of talking one is capable of, the more choices one can make and solutions one can invent.

Meaning is in people. The more meanings one has in his experience, the more new meanings he can generate or acquire.

The level of abstraction at which one uses language in any context is an index of the extent to which one is 'in touch' with reality. The higher the level, the less is the contact with reality. (Postman and Weingartner 1969).

In the next chapter we use the perspective that this provides to look harder at differences within the culturing process.

Further reading
Postman and Weingartner (1969) provide a very readable introduction to this area, though the polemical tone of their book now seems irrelevant. Hoggart's (1973) low key, thoughtful approach is a useful antidote. Books by Cassirer (e.g. 1944) are neither easy to get nor easy to read, but are valuable in presenting the issues in a wide philosophical context. For an accessible review of psychological research on the processing of experience see Bruner (1974).

5 FORMS OF EXPERIENCE AND CULTURAL GROWTH

It is possible to accept the argument developed in chapter 4 that symbolic forms and systems have a central function in culture, but to regard it as a matter of philosophical rather than practical import. But the point *is* practical, because it enables several controversial issues in curriculum planning to be restated and approached differently.

(1) Symbolic systems and the structure of the curriculum

We noted in chapter 2 that it is possible to complain that the division of experience into different categories or 'subjects' (art, craft, religion; science, recreation, etc.) is artificial, and to say that it devalues the unity and spontaneity of ordinary-life experience. It is possible to attribute this fragmentation of experience to social control, which enshrines some forms of knowledge. It can be suggested that high status is accorded to some forms of experience and low status to others. Mixed forms of experience, such as management, technology, or teaching, where theory and practice meet, may seem to threaten the 'purity' of enshrined ways of conceiving life such as law, science, fine arts, and the power of those people versed in them. However, to acknowledge the way in which symbolic forms differ (for example, mathematical notations and religious imagery) is to accept that there are modes of

48

experience which are radically different in kind. It also seems inevitable that groups of people will develop interests in these different modes of experience and that 'traditions' or communities of work and study in them will grow up.

It is also clear that some ways of shaping experience, notably in the sciences, can be analysed and differentiated in terms of (1) their basic concepts (for example, valency in chemistry, marginal utility in economics), (2) the logical structures by which concepts are related (theories, models, schema, etc.), (3) the ways in which statements are tested against experience, and (4) methodologies and strategies for exploring experience. The cogency of this analysis when applied to science has led to a strong emphasis in curriculum upon *conceptual structure* (Bruner 1960 and 1966). Because 'subjects' tend to be equated with the traditions of enquiry that have developed generative symbolic systems, this has tended to underwrite the organisation of curriculum by 'subjects'.

The most influential arguments about curriculum organisation are those of Hirst (1965) and Hirst and Peters (1970), who stress the central importance of separate and irreducible 'disciplines' of knowledge, distinguished by their symbolic structures and criteria for establishing truths. The curriculum implications and limitations of this position are considered again in chapter 10, and in greater detail by Skilbeck (1975) in Open University Course E203, Unit 4. Our view is this: if schools think about how they can *use* the 'disciplines' of knowledge in order to mediate culture (rather than teach the 'disciplines' as such), then 'disciplines' make an essential contribution to the curriculum without dominating its organisation. There are obviously many central aspects of life where the propositional truths developed by 'disciplines' have little direct relevance: experience in which we make judgements about complex situations, interact or sympathise with other people, enjoy recreation, landscapes, music, and so on. However, curricula built on the basis of these aspects of life are likely to be trivial and intellectually dissatisfying unless they are linked with the more penetrative ways of viewing life developed through the quest for truth, for knowledge rather than opinion. The central curriculum task is to relate these penetrative ('disciplined') ways of experiencing to children's general flow of consciousness.

Chanan and Gilchrist (1974, especially chapter 6) get to the heart of the matter. They stress the crucial function of symbolic forms in developing children's ability to achieve focus in complex experience, to hold relationships in mind, and to think about their flexibility. To develop this overall capacity children need the opportunity to detach themselves from experience which demands continuous direct responses. Detached from the day-to-day compulsions of living we can become conscious of key symbolic forms, refine and extend their use, criticise their use and consider alternatives. An essential cultural role of universities and traditions of disinterested enquiry and scholarship is that they enable some adults to do this throughout their lives. An essential cultural role of schools is that they enable children to experience a detached 'culturing system' through which they can come to use symbolic forms critically and self-consciously. But there can be no hard line drawn between the symbols we use in detached, bounded aspects of life and those of untidy ordinary life. We obviously can draw to some extent upon ways of thinking developed in science, art, history, etc., in family life, at work, watching television, etc. But the extent depends on the practice and encouragement that we get in schools to *coordinate* detached, reflective ways of using symbols with day-to-day experience and action.

The practical issue of curriculum planning can be summarised thus: how can the traditional selection of formalised culture (the subject structures around which secondary schools are organised and through which teachers are educated) be coordinated with children's ways of thinking (which are better reflected by the popular culture of newspapers, television and by youth culture)? Are there potential common elements in their hidden culturing processes? Can we find common denominators in both the detached, critical use of symbols which underlie the stylised outcomes of the sciences, arts and humanities; and in the everyday thought and feeling of ordinary people? The answer is that there are similarities in the ways that both forms of culture mediate and structure experience, though their dominant images and techniques may differ significantly. Above all their procedures for establishing precision of meaning and truth may differ. But both can make use of broadly comparable strategies for solving problems; both *can* illustrate the importance of discrimination of meanings, mutual criticism, new metaphors, evaluative standards, etc. However, these potential common denominators in differing cultural processes must first be recognised and thought out in curriculum planning. Then they can be systematically articulated in lesson planning and classroom transaction (see chapters 9 and 10; see also Stenhouse 1967, chapters 6 to 9).

We return here to the central idea of the *mediation* of culture through awareness of symbolic forms and the different contexts of their use. The shift in orientation from that embodied in much curriculum thinking is significant and bears restating slightly differently:

What matters about traditional schooling's neglect of . . . contemporary culture is . . . that it has meant a sustained antagonism towards the primary terms in which pupils conceive the world themselves . . . The error was not that one form of culture was effectively upheld at the expense of another (for pupils still *experienced* the world in terms of their own images) but that, failing to acknowledge and accommodate contemporary culture as realised in the consciousness of living individuals, schooling failed to convey meaningfully the additional cultural resources in which it specialised. It neglected the *relationship* between current and enshrined elements of the same culture and, therefore, failed to restore the enshrined elements to real currency. (Chanan and Gilchrist 1974)

(2) Symbolic forms, cultural intervention and classroom culture

It does not require a long spell of teaching experience to realise that it is difficult to apply the approach just described in actual classroom situations. Pupil expectations and lack of facility in formal discussion, discipline problems and class size, all provide good reasons for retaining a subject-based, chalk-and-talk or worksheet approach. There is not space here to discuss the various teaching strategies and techniques of questioning which help to overcome these difficulties. In any case, the effect of classroom techniques may be transient unless they are related to the wider social and longer-term temporal contexts of curriculum – what we have described as cultural projects.

The following extract from a much longer transcript of classroom discussion in a class using Schools Council Humanities Project materials helps to set the scene. There are thirteen boys, average age fourteen years, discussing 'Men and Marriage'.

BOY A: Well, I think you'd do better to get married, 'cos . . . I should think it would complicate things, you know, like getting a job and that sort of thing.

BOY B: Why? . . .

BOY A: . . . It's just the way things are isn't it?

BOY B: I don't see how any complications can arise in getting a job through not being married.

BOY C: Well, surely it's more economical to get married because if you're living with somebody you're still a bachelor, therefore you have to pay taxes for a bachelor, which works out more expensive than if you're married.

(4 seconds silence)

TEACHER: You made a point a moment ago, you asked a question, 'Why get married?' Let's throw it open. What do the rest of you feel?

BOY D: You get married because you love somebody, don't you?

BOY E: You get married because you think if you didn't people would talk.

BOY F: It's true, most people are scared of not getting married because of what the neighbours would say.

BOY B: I found this.

BOY A: Who cares what the neighbours say?

BOY E: That's my opinion, but . . . most people care a great deal about what the neighbours think about. . .

BOY A: Well, you live for yourselves, not for the neighbours.

BOY E: True, but some people still have that outlook..

BOY A: Yes, well if they are only getting married because they think of what the neighbours would say, there's no point in getting married at all, is there?

BOY B: Well, because their mothers and fathers got married. . .

BOY A: . . . got no reason. . .

BOY B: . . . and their grandmothers and fathers. . .

BOY A: . . . because it's the . . . done thing. . .

(Hamingson 1973)

The environment for the exploration and coordination of

53

ideas is favourable: over many months the boys have got accustomed to critical discussion; they are seated in an informal group. Even so, the exchange is neither fluent nor sophisticated. On the face of it, it lacks the detached focusing upon experience which it is claimed that the formal disciplines of enquiry can provide. But even when this ideal is realised in universities (which it often is not), it is usually the outcome of a lengthy, protected and leisurely initiation into conventions of mannered analytic discourse. Moreover, it is discourse which generally avoids such emotionally charged matters as marriage.

In the discussion the boys are moving, albeit slowly, towards a shared focus upon the conceptions and expectations suggested by the idea of marriage, towards a recovery of the funded experience for which the word provides a shorthand. They are doing so in a way which could not be replaced by giving them formal definitions of marriage, and explanations of the interdependence of institutions, human needs and moral traditions. The form of the discussion achieves something which no 'transmission' of ideas about marriage can do. It makes visible the relationship between symbolic forms on the one hand, and, on the other hand, the conventions that give them significance, and people's beliefs and values.

Because experiencing is embedded in words like marriage, work, education, etc., we seldom consider how they *represent* (or 'codify') experience. The Spanish philosopher Ortega Y Gasset expressed the problem as follows: 'We find ourselves amongst a network of ready made solutions . . . are constantly receiving collective convictions [of other generations] before we have become aware of the problems for which they are supposed to be solutions . . . The very language in which we think . . . is itself an alien way of thinking, a collective philosophy' (Ortega 1959).

Our concern with the extract is to crystallise further the idea of teaching as the mediation of culture, and to show the sense in which it is cultural intervention. It is often justifiably a process of helping children to 'unlearn' or, better, reinterpret, some of the basic modes of experiencing that they have formed in their earliest years at home. Something more than belief in either techniques of questioning and the systematic promotion of children's skills, or romanticism about creativity, 'discovery methods' and the unfolding of children's capacities is needed. Some important manipulative and perceptual skills, such as writing and word recognition, can only be learnt by systematic practice. Equally, the disposition to make intelligent guesses, empathise with others or develop imaginative ideas can only be fostered by actively encouraging them. But the teacher's role as mediator of culture is none of these. Part of it is the long-term task of cultivating, or culturing, a medium of shared understandings; in other words, a classroom culture through which the relationship between symbolic forms and reality can be articulated, explored, criticised, refined, and, equally important, sustained.

The point can be underlined by reconsidering the story of Helen Keller. In the transformation of her capacity to experience life she not only acquired access to finger language. Nobody is changed by language or any system for mediating experience unless they also acquire the conventions of usage which enable the symbolic system to work. In other words, to share in forms of culture is to know how the rules implicit in them focus our attention on particular aspects of experience. Both Helen Keller and her teacher implicitly accepted a common set of rules for the focusing and coordinating of experience. There was an interlocking of meanings, as between lock and key. The point is that the dramatic effect of Helen's use of symbols (the 'key') can only be fully understood in relation to Mrs Sullivan's response, her congruent interpretation (the 'lock'). The slowly developed relationship between the one and the other, in their sharing of common conventions of meaning, was really more significant

55

than the particular breakthrough in Helen's capacity to process experience.

(3) Cultural currency and cultural growth

Is it possible to say what constitutes a rich culture, whether it is a classroom, school, regional, or national culture? The answer is: not as such, because, as we have seen, culture is not really a thing, an entity, at all. To talk of a rich or impoverished culture would inevitably oversimplify a complex and dynamic process of interaction between symbols, social relationships, and beliefs and values. But we can certainly look at the quality of a nation's, school's or family's culturing processes; at whether its members are aware of gaps between what they claim to believe and value and what they in fact do, of inconsistencies between what they claim to know and their management of their environment. There is something amiss with our culturing processes if we know that we are dissipating our natural resources, but lack the will to plan, educate and regulate social life accordingly.

One way of considering the quality of culture is to examine its dominant symbolic forms. What words, theories, rituals, images, do people most use? This leads us to ask what gives 'currency' to symbolic forms? What enables us to trade experience, to have confidence that our words, actions or other expressions will bring about an appropriate response in others, a reciprocal focusing of their attention to experience? The answer is that if particular symbolic and expressive forms are to attain currency, then people have to come to use those forms with recurrent discrimination. For example, we distinguish between 'good' and 'bad' writing by criteria of whether it appeals to sentiment or sensibility, to moral thought or to moralising; whether it coarsens experience by using clichés or sharpens perception by articulating shades of meaning.

Nowadays institutions such as schools, the BBC, newspapers, etc., can do much to enhance or weaken such use. Their coy, interchangeable use of such concepts as girl-friend, mistress, natural wife, lover, etc., is a negative example. Their recently more frank discussion of industrial disputes and mental health is a positive example. But the discriminating recurrent use of symbolic forms requires face-to-face or other two-way interaction between people if symbolic forms are both to evoke common experience and relate ideas to feeling and action. For example, we have noted how little language there is for talking about education which is both clear and evocative.

The limitation of newspapers and television (and expository teaching) in the culturing process is that you cannot answer them back. Because they only 'transmit', they provide no milieu which fosters an active response through reflection on how far their use of symbolic forms is congruent with your own experience. For this reason symbols which were originally subtle and discriminating become debased. The misuse of Bernstein's bold but speculative theorising on language codes is a case in point (Rosen 1972). The danger that new usages which distinguish unacknowledged aspects of experience will never achieve currency is as great. There is a saying amongst scientists that new theories never can gain recognition until the authors of earlier theories have retired or died.

At first hearing this seems to discount the central value of impartial weighing of evidence in science, of objectivity, knowledge of the 'real' world. Rather it is to reinterpret conceptions of objectivity and knowledge; it is to think of knowledge less as something 'out there', than as something created through the speculative imagination of scientists, artists, historians, etc., and complementary processes of verification and criticism within a community of shared assumptions. Sometimes, however, these assumptions are challenged as new symbolic systems are developed. As Medawar (1969) points out, some of the most important aspects of scientists' thinking are embodied in comments such as:

What gave you the idea of trying . . . ?
I'm taking the view that the underlying mechanism is. . .
My results don't make a story yet.
What happens if you assume that . . . ?

There are many powerful trends in society, such as those which ensue indirectly from technological change, which affect the currency of forms of culture without our awareness. Raymond Williams described how the Industrial Revolution radically changed the aspects of experience that people associated with words such as 'industry', 'democracy', 'class', 'art' and 'culture' itself. With the disruption of community and rural life, the last of these came to mean 'the general body of the arts' or a 'whole way of life' (Williams 1950). As a consequence, a way of talking about important facets of experience became devalued.

Our concern here is the practical implication of the 'currency' metaphor for curriculum. A first implication is that it enables us to distinguish between how culture may unthinkingly give symbolic forms currency, and how it may consciously reject, adapt and improve them. Curriculum planning which aims to show children how to coordinate different forms of experiencing considers both.

The difference between the informal processes by which symbolic forms become adopted in popular use and the more formal processes by which they gain acceptance within academic disciplines is not always clear cut. Symbolic forms cannot themselves be tested to see if they are true, whether they are congruent with an 'outer reality'. We cannot ask whether idioms of expression in the arts, or the concepts of gravity, the novel, or social structure, are in themselves true. But the cultural conventions of the academic disciplines require that clear propositions or judgements be derived from symbolic forms and that they be stringently evaluated. Within many academic disciplines it is not possible to do this in strictly scientific terms, because quantification and prediction are inappropriate. But in academic life the users of symbolic forms, such as historians, philosophers or theologians, are pressed to point to evidence which supports their representations of experience. Critics compare their outcomes with those of alternative representations.

We less frequently open up popular or 'common sense' ways of interpreting life to critical evaluation, because we take for granted their most basic assumptions and metaphors. Hence too much popular discussion of current affairs, morality, the arts, veers dissatisfyingly between dogmatic assertion and fatalistic recourse to the cliché that 'It's all a matter of opinion'. But this need not be so. As we saw earlier, the differences between formal and informal evaluations of experience spring from the differing degrees of detachment and involvement in action. Many areas of social life neglected in curriculum, such as work and politics, demand alternations of detachment and action.

Here we reach what is probably the most difficult conception to grasp in this book – a conception to be reflected on and struggled with if we claim to understand culture. It is a conception of the role in education of:

the problematisation of the world of work, products, ideas, convictions, aspirations, myths, arts, science; the world in short of culture and history which is the result of the relations between human beings and the world. To present this human world as a problem for human beings is to propose that they 'enter into' it critically, taking the operation as a whole, their action and that of others on it. It means 're-entering into' the world through the 'entering into' of the previous understandings which may have been arrived at naively because reality was not examined as a whole. In 'entering into' their own world, people become aware of their manner of acquiring knowledge and then realise the need to know even more. (Freire 1973, pp. 154-5)

We can illustrate the idea of 'problematisation' by applying it to our own problem, that of deciding what experience should be provided in the curriculum. There is a problem about what we really mean by seeing it as 'a selection from the culture of a society' (Lawton 1973). It helps sharper thinking to ask: Does 'culture' refer primarily to the *outcomes* or products of people's shared feelings, thoughts, actions and communicating (for example, the explicit knowledge, and beliefs in traditions, rules of conduct, books, etc.)? Or does 'culture' direct attention more to the underlying often hidden *processes* of shared feeling, thought, etc.? The significance of the cultural product/process distinction has already been made (chapter 4), but a simplified example will help. It is salutary to recognise that science is part of the culture, from which we select, but is our main curriculum interest in the transmission of the outcomes of science, its systems of laws and facts which constitute knowledge of universal applicability? Most science teachers would say that they are also concerned with the transmission of procedures to establish facts and scientific laws, its processes of experimental design, validation of hypotheses, etc. But are these the same as cultural processes in science?

Cultural processes in science reside in what scientists actually feel, think and do as scientists. There is more to them than the formal 'scientific' procedures and concepts emphasised in many school curricula. These rules of scientific grammar are crucial in regulating research and in presenting its findings, but the living processes of science are embodied equally in the *informal* discussion and social interaction amongst working groups of scientists. It is the ebb and flow of criticism, witticism, interest and disinterest, which induces them to regard some aspects of experience and

60

problems as more significant than others. The way in which people, ideas and actions interact in this milieu prompts them to revise and discard ideas and disposes them to perceive particular thoughts and feelings as scientific or unscientific. This is at the heart of the experience of science as culture, though it appears in no science textbook or research paper.

Our initial question was how the culturing processes of the school can both reflect and enhance those of the environing society. We reinterpreted the question to ask how the more detached, disinterested ways of using symbolic forms in which schools and universities specialise should relate to the more powerful and consequential systems of thought and action in economic life and popular culture. By implication, we are asking how to decide whether curriculum development counts as cultural development.

The culture provided by the curriculum can be said to 'grow' when teachers provide widening access to the range of symbolic forms, including their use in systems of action, but it is equally necessary that teachers have developed the relationships with one another which enable them to sustain, criticise and extend their usage of these symbolic and expressive forms. However, we cannot leave these fostering social relationships to men's natural goodwill. Symbolic forms have a double-edged function: they enable us to demarcate and maintain the boundaries between different interest groups' experience of the world, as well as to share it. Thus cultural growth in curriculum depends upon a relaxed and continuous exchange of ideas amongst teachers which prevents curriculum boundaries from becoming rigid and insulated from alternative views.

The day-to-day pressures of school life and the need for stability and professional security often lead originally innovative curriculum programmes to become stylised and devoid of critical consciousness. But the sustaining of a milieu of critical consciousness in schools is not impracticable when the arts of imparting and diversifying culture are consciously linked with the conception of curriculum planning outlined in chapter 2.

This is a corporate task for the school, not one for the individual teacher. It reflects the truth that the currency and discriminating power of symbolic forms, and the relationships between people, are two sides of the same coin.

Summary
We have argued in this chapter that to mediate culture involves being conscious of symbolic systems, and of whether they are being used so as to discriminate or conflate aspects of experience; but this is to acknowledge that the sustaining and development of distinctions of meaning depends on the stability and milieu of criticism that institutions provide. This can be put another way: the conventions through which schools approach and regulate their overall task of curriculum planning are as much part of the culturing process as classroom teaching itself.

Further reading
There are three writers referred to in this chapter of whose work you need first-hand knowledge: Hirst (1975), Freire (1973) and Chanan and Gilchrist (1974). All will repay the close study that their arguments demand. Stenhouse (1967) is much easier to read, but writes with no less insight. Skilbeck in Unit 3 of The Open University (1975) makes a more detailed analysis of different ways of classifying knowledge and experience.

The point made in the last section of the chapter about the crucial role of a community of shared assumptions in the development of testable or 'scientific' knowledge merits further study. It is lucidly discussed in a short, inexpensive book on Karl Popper, the eminent philosopher of science, by

Magee (1973); and in greater philosophic depth by Toulmin (1972). Its implications for science curricula are presented by Tawney (1974) in a form that even non-scientists will find illuminating.

6 VALUES, BELIEFS AND CULTURE

As we have seen in preceding chapters, culture impinges upon the curriculum in many different ways. The teacher, unavoidably and inescapably, is a bearer of meanings and values, and these he mediates through his teaching. The pupils, too, live in a cultural world both outside and inside school. Even within the school, important differences of perception, values and actions may be observed when comparing classroom behaviour with behaviour in the playground, in school outings and so on.

In this chapter we shall be considering ways in which the school curriculum might be structured with reference to broader social aims and values. We shall be using terms such as 'ideology' and 'indoctrination', which are apt to make teachers and parents uneasy, with their political overtones and the suggestion that perhaps schools are to be involved in shaping the social and political order. As we shall see there is a sense in which education, if it is doing its job properly, is subversive of certain customs, beliefs and institutions in society. But this is not at all the same thing as investing teachers and schools with the right to pursue and impose particular political doctrines.

Why should education be thought to have a subversive role at all? Are not educational institutions designed by society – and financed and staffed – to transmit established values, skills, knowledge and techniques, from the older to the younger generation? Is not the curriculum simply a practical plan or scheme for the guidance of teachers in their task of transmission? We have seen already that the idea of transmission is not as simple as it appears at first sight. Necessarily, the teacher selects, chooses, makes judgements about, rejects, places in order of priority – all processes to which the *transmission* metaphor does less than justice.

On a broader plane, the curriculum is only partially constituted by subject matter, selected by objective criteria and divided up into units or lessons for which slots must be found on the timetable. The curriculum is this, but, as we have seen, it is much more besides. Curriculum construction, whether in tightly defined subjects, as in the upper years of secondary education, or in broadly defined interdisciplinary units, in the earlier years of schooling, raises fundamental questions about culture and experience. Although he may not always be conscious of doing so, by his choices for inclusion and exclusion and by his mode of communicating these choices through his teaching, the teacher makes judgements about what is desirable in the experience and growth of his pupils. In principle, at least, he has the power to undermine some aspects of the culture and to strengthen others. It was this understanding that led the philosopher, Fichte, to call upon the teachers and the schools to lead the German people in a struggle against the occupying armies of Napoleon. Fichte's vision of a new education may lead you to think of the uses made of education for propagandist purposes and its submission to political doctrines in some countries. There are dangers, yet they cannot be resisted by closing our eyes to the functions that schools do exercise or the power that teachers can and do have at their disposal. Note, however, that Fichte's language seems as much religious as political:

The means of salvation which I promised to indicate consists in the fashioning of an entirely new self, which may have existed before, perhaps in individuals as an exception, but never as a universal and national self, and in the education of the nation, whose former life has died out and become the supplement of an alien elite, to a completely new life . . . In a word, it is a total change of the existing system of education that I propose as the sole means of preserving the existence of the German nation. (Fichte, 1922, pp. 12-13)

Many contemporary instances of a similar conception of education might be cited, from countries like Tanzania, Israel, China, India and Cuba. Admittedly, all are new nations in the sense that some far-reaching political change has occurred and education has been assigned a task it seldom if ever appears to have in non-revolutionary societies. The culture modifying role of education may be observed much more clearly in these new states. Yet it is also at work in more stable societies, even if the complexity of the cultural situations within which schools and teachers work, and the wide range of options that appear to be open to them, make it difficult to see just what is going on.

If we consider that the task facing the school and the teacher includes the selection of curriculum content, we may appreciate that cultural choices are being made and that the possibility of culture modification is not as fanciful as it may sound at first. In subjects such as history, religious studies, social studies, geography and English images are being communicated, responses invited, sensibilities and insights encouraged, values fostered — or challenged. History is a good illustration, since every nation presents through its history textbooks, its teacher training processes, its examination syllabuses, and in more subtle ways through discourse amongst historians and teachers, basic views about its own past. These views contribute to the formation of individual and national identity. They may even, as is the case in Northern Ireland in Catholic and Protestant schools, contri-

66

bute to some extent to the formation of separate subcultural identities.

Suppose teachers of history began – as they might – to focus on the historical perspectives developed in other cultures, on the idea of an international or transnational social order, on the arts and the sciences instead of political, military and social events. It is not difficult to envisage a very different view of any given society emerging in pupils' minds from a drastic reordering of what is to count as 'history'. In practice, of course, all kinds of constraints operate to prevent this from happening, or to mute its effect where individual teachers and schools try something radically different. However, the point here is that decisions, even within the boundaries of single disciplines, do presuppose and project particular cultural images and values.

The example of history, or of subject matter generally in the humanities and social sciences, might be accepted as obvious enough. But it is not only in socially and politically sensitive areas of the curriculum that culturally significant choices are made by teachers in their everyday work. The shaping of pupil experience, their awareness of what the world is and what it might be like – these fundamental elements in individual and national identity are affected by the manner in which any subject matter is presented, by the teacher's personality and mode of operation in the classroom, the rules of the school, the messages conveyed through the common rituals of assembly and speechday, the informal world of the playground, etc. (see also chapter 3).

Many teachers are well aware that the curriculum decisions they take – or have made for them – raise issues about their beliefs and cultural role. They sometimes wish that 'politics' could be taken out of education. It is important to ask why some political and social reformers take such a close interest in education and whether we should try to 'depoliticise' curriculum questions. Politics has to do with the distribution, exercise and justification of power in society.

'Power' in this context refers to the capacity and resource to pursue and achieve ends and purposes, held by certain groups, and to deflect, thwart or conciliate other groups pursuing different ends and purposes. As we have seen, curriculum questions are not restricted to technical problems, such as the teaching of a particular skill. Inevitably curriculum questions raise problems about social values, the needs and interests of different groups in society, and the social meaning and significance of knowledge itself, including knowledge in the physical sciences (e.g. is the *content* of physical science courses wholly separable from the *uses* to which physical science knowledge is put in society?) Is it surprising, then, that the curriculum of a universal institution, the school, should be seen to have a political as well as a pedagogical dimension? Is it not a matter of common sense to seek to understand how the curriculum is and may be put to political use rather than to protest – ineffectively – against the intrusion of politics into education?

Several of the contributors to the *Black Papers* have recognised that many of the changes taking place in or proposed for education have important political connotations. Generally, they have attacked the child-centrism of progressive education, the philosophy of the modern primary school, and the comprehensive institution of secondary education. Not all of these writers, however, appear to appreciate that in advocating increased competition (in which many will fail), fixed standards (which the majority will not succeed in attaining), equality of opportunity (but not equality of treatment or provision) and various other qualities and goals, they are sustaining a political programme. There is a dangerous naivety about attacks on the 'progressive syndrome', 'insidious' social engineering through education, and 'egalitarianism' which does not squarely face up to the social and political implications of what is termed, tendentiously, 'the fight for education'.

This is not to deny that *Black Paper* authors are fighting to maintain educational, social and political values which they hold to firmly and for which they can master strong arguments. But it is no less important for this action group to affirm its own cultural stance including its politics than to denounce the cultural position of its opponents, criticising them for adopting a political programme. That is what it, also, has as one of its foundations. Thus grammar schools are defended by *Black Paper* authors as 'good' schools (which, in some cases, no one would deny they are) and comprehensives are attacked for their shortcomings (which, like all schools, they have). But grammar schools, and their curricula, are an important facet of a powerful subculture which has its traditions, its values, its way of life, and their 'goodness' is not merely a pedagogical matter; it consists partly in that they serve the interests of the subculture.

Likewise, as the *Black Paper* authors correctly note, comprehensive schools express the values and aim to serve the interests of various groups in our society. Their efforts to develop integrated studies, to de-stream, to build up a common curriculum, reflect not merely pedagogical concern but a broader social and political philosophy. It would make for greater clarity and honesty in debates to accept that the arguments about forms of schooling and types of curricula are both cultural and irreducibly political. There are tensions, disagreements and dilemmas in our culture, many of them the consequence of a long history of social stratification, economic inequality and status difference. It would be very odd if we could proceed to any depth in the analysis of curriculum decision making without encountering these differences.

Amongst contemporary educational theorists, Professor G. H. Bantock has been the least equivocal in his assertion both of the cultural context within which decisions must be taken and the separate educational paths that should be followed in educating minorities and masses. Bantock values tradition and for him this means understanding the deep gulf that exists between the few and the many. The latter, guided by custom and habit, have their roots in a non-literate rural community: their qualities are those of 'keen observation', 'direct sensuous awareness', 'clarity', 'steadfastness', 'stability' – and a certain narrowness. They possessed – as did society as a whole – 'unconscious harmonies' until the onset of industrialisation and urbanisation (Bantock 1968). The minority, on the other hand, are distinguished by a heightened consciousness, a high degree of literacy, intellectual interests and attainments and, perhaps, spiritual superiority (Bantock 1970). To the one, Bantock attributes a folk culture which is communicative but essentially non-literate; to the other, a high culture which is orientated towards 'mind knowledge' and the more sophisticated levels and aspects of the symbolic systems through which this knowledge is to be communicated and transmitted.

While it would be an oversimplification of Professor Bantock's position to say that he would be satisfied to divide the school curriculum into two distinct parts, each corresponding to these separate cultures, his thinking definitely moves in this direction. He is deeply disturbed by what he sees as the corruption of folk values and by the breakdown in modern industrial society of an overall unity which binds together in a mutually supporting relationship these two cultures. Whilst he does not suggest that adequate educational programmes could be developed just by a process of distillation from what is 'best' in the two cultures, the reader is left with the impression that Professor Bantock would like to retain what would be, in essence, two distinct forms of schooling, different in purpose, in curriculum, in institutional setting and in outcome.

Our purpose is to draw attention to the social and political dimensions of what is presented as pedagogical theory. For Professor Bantock, a stable society appears preferable to one in constant change; basic decisions about social structures and the political system seem, in his theory, to belong as if by

70

right to the highly educated, those brought up to a deep sense of the past and its values. He is hostile to the dominance of our institutions by economic and commercial considerations, and to what he takes to be the philosophies – notably American pragmatism – derived from the businessman's practical way of doing things. Broadly speaking he draws a distinction between education that is practical, vocational, geared to socioeconomic efficiency and based on a generally instrumental view of life, and that which is humanistic, intellectualistic, and based on the cultivation of taste: sensibility and the moral and intellectual virtues. Historically, his view is part of the aristocratic-humanistic tradition which derives from some parts of the Platonic philosophy and found its sharper expression in some parts of the English public and grammar school systems. In the language we shall be using in this book, his position is no less ideological than are the educational theories advanced in communist and developing third world nations.

It is misleading to equate 'culture' with 'high culture', i.e. the style, outlook, language uses, tastes and interests of particular groups, mainly those educated in the arts and humanities. In earlier chapters we saw that culture is essentially process. Its understanding requires us to examine the meanings which men develop in and through social interactions. Thus conceived, culture is in no way distinctive of any one group or class in society, and to talk of 'high' culture is to talk of only one cultural subset. Moreover, the use of the qualifier 'high' is a valuation: the culture in question is being rated higher than others. Are we entitled to make such a judgement? When the expression 'high culture' is used, is too much taken for granted about the worth of one set of cultural experiences?

These questions raise value issues. Education is a value-saturated process. This is so because the value judgements of the teacher, of the educational authorities and of the public at large impinge upon and structure the life of the school.

Inevitably, the learner's value judgements are affected, although this is by no means a one-way, uniform process, since the learner moves in other spheres in addition to the school and is frequently more affected by the values of, say, the world of football spectatorship, popular music, comics and magazines than of the school itself. To recognise this fact need not lead us to accept the view that the discussion of values in relation to schooling is a waste of time. Schools will remain an obligatory part of children's experience of growing up for a very long time to come. We must, then, consider the kinds of approaches which it is open to a teacher to adopt when thinking about his role as mediator and interpreter of values.

There are many moral values which, at a high level of generality, it will be agreed that schools should foster. These include integrity, honesty and considerateness. But it is doubtful whether a very long list of moral values could be agreed upon. When such a list is presented for comment, different groups rank the values differently. What matters about statements of general values is how they are interpreted; how the values are coordinated and expressed in courses of action. For example, compare a term like 'integrity', which may mean very different things in different cultures. However, there are less obvious differences within a given society and teachers need to be sensitive to these differences and ought not to assume that their own values will be unconsciously shared or appreciated by the pupils, even when the same words, like 'honesty' or 'truthfulness' may be used in conversation between teachers and pupils.

Questions about the relationship between a teacher's own values and those he promotes in his teaching are unavoidable. He could decide to be fairly rigid himself about a moral code, but could opt to promote wide-ranging enquiry amongst his pupils, enabling and encouraging them to make up their own minds. In effect this is the approach advocated in the Humanities Curriculum Project where teachers are

72

encouraged to adopt a neutralist classroom stance whilst stimulating their pupils to review problems and issues, to make up their own minds about them (Humanities Curriculum Project, 1970). However, the values of the teacher are unlikely to be held in check by this technique, since values operate unconsciously as well as consciously. They affect not only the explicit choice of subject matter for teaching and the techniques of communication, discussion, debate, etc., that may be adopted. Personal teaching style is a complex which includes mannerisms, asides, moods, gestures and spontaneous responses. Interpersonal relationships in and out of the classroom, between teachers and taught, also affect the learning climate. Thus a teacher's values are likely to pervade his teaching even when he strives to make them conscious and to limit their impact. It is for this reason that it is important for teachers to reflect on their values and to spend time trying to analyse, justify and modify their value positions. Teacher education is not only a matter of building up knowledge structures and acquiring techniques. It should be no less directed at value inquiry.

Thought about the needs of the learner raises several possibilities for value education. What do we want pupils to learn, and under what conditions and circumstances do we want them to learn? Do we value pupil freedom, in the sense that what we are aiming for is a pupil who is intellectually free, mature and balanced in his judgements, capable of growing in his own self-knowledge? Admittedly, these are very generalised expressions, and to make them more concrete we have to relate them to particular activities and processes. In British education where all round individual growth is usually rated highly by teachers who are asked to rank their general aims, generalisations about pupil autonomy will sound familiar enough. But even within this society disagreements and differences emerge when we try to pin down these generalisations to particular freedoms for pupils in the school environment (Free to choose the time and place for learning? Free to select the themes and topics to study?).

Through these freedoms we could create conditions for learning which maximise the pupil's choices; strengthen his capacity to deliberate, choose, compare, discriminate; and provide opportunities for him to make his own value judgements; develop his own life style. One of the weaknesses of much of our schooling, particularly at the secondary stage, is the unwillingness or inability of schools to face up to the short-term, practical implications of the longer-term aims they proclaim. Values remain lofty, noble and remote unless seen as the *processes* of schooling themselves: what teachers actually do, and how the curriculum is organised.

Summary
Let us sum up. If teachers are to do this job of value education honestly, they have to consider the specific values which are embedded in ways of life. In discussing Professor Bantock's views, we saw that traditionalists are very conscious of the threat to the values and particular life styles posed by the reorganisation of schooling and the attempt to introduce common cultural cores to the curriculum. Advocates of these changes are often vague about the mode of life that they would like to see emerging through these changes. What are the emerging values of a democratic, egalitarian, populist society? How are minority interests sustained within these mass movements? How different would these curricula be from those which we find in our present, still divided school system? By taking an interest in discussions about the future shape of our school system and the content of teaching, teachers can retain their own professional freedom. Moreover, participation in curriculum construction and class-discussion is the best means to clarify one's own value position; and hence to reduce the gap between classroom realities and educational policy making.

Further reading
See Cox and Boyson (1975) for examples of the value position embodied in the latest *Black Papers*; and Skilbeck in Unit
4 of The Open University (1975) for further counter-
arguments and clarification of the role of values in curriculum.

7 IDEOLOGY AND CULTURE

The word *ideology* is both less familiar than *value* to teachers and more threatening in its overtones. In this chapter we shall endeavour to show that the concept of ideology, carefully used, helps to analyse the cultural role of the school. There are ideological issues and questions in schooling which teachers might be more aware of than they generally are at present. But we must first strip the word 'ideology' of some of its particular political associations. Ideology is in fact a feature of all societies, not specifically of those of a totalitarian character. True, ideological debates are much more acrimonious and ideological programmes more conspicuous in societies undergoing rapid change and political revolutions than in more stable societies. But it would be a mistake to suppose that education in more settled traditional societies such as Britain and other western democracies is somehow less 'ideological' than it is in, say, China or the new African countries.

This point will become clear from a consideration of what ideologies are. An ideology is a system or a cluster of beliefs and values held by social groups which help to bind those groups together and are used by them to further their own interests. Looked at more closely, ideologies are seen to contain beliefs and doctrines concerning man and his place in the world, the social and political structures in which he wishes to live, and his views about how best to achieve his ends and purposes. That is, ideologies are both complex and action-orientated. They are not restricted in content to any one point or area of the political spectrum, and they may be religious, aesthetic, metaphysical, economic or political in tendency. Thus it makes sense to talk about the ideology of American democracy, of the French bourgeoisie, of Chinese Maoists, of Tanzanian socialists – or of the English middle class. Ideologies may characterise whole societies or even whole periods in history, or they may be specific to subcultures within a given society.

Why is the concept of ideology so important for educators and what has it to do with culture analysis? Taking the second question first, we may think of culture, from an ideological standpoint, in a number of ways:

(1) Ideology may be a movement within culture, clustering values and beliefs, organising them into an action programme, and proclaiming this action programme noisily and persistently.

(2) Cultural experience, which may be very diverse and varied, can influence the manner in which ideologies are developed, transmitted over time and space – e.g. communism means different things within the different cultural traditions of the various nations of Europe, east and west.

(3) Within a given culture there may be a number of competing and conflicting ideologies at work – e.g. in Britain there is a clash between the grammar/public school ideology and egalitarianism.

(4) Culture will be viewed and interpreted from within particular ideological frameworks; hence the disagreements about the significance of particular cultural traditions – e.g. the disputes about what is most characteristic of and worthwhile about the cultural traditions of liberalism in Britain, some treating it as

77

the foundation of *laissez-faire* politics and others as the justification for interventionism.

It should now be apparent why the concept of ideology is important for teachers even if the word itself is not part of everyday educational language. Teachers work within the ideological framework of a given society and they are under pressure from various groups in that society to transmit to pupils the values and beliefs of that ideology. Some teachers opposed to the prevailing ideology of their society may feel inclined to propagate the values and beliefs of the particular ideology to which they subscribe, whether this be religious or political. The number of overt ideological clashes within the education profession seems to be increasing and some teachers and heads have found themselves in conflict with school managers and governors, local authorities and the voluntary bodies which have responsibility for certain schools.

There is another use of the word 'ideology' which occurs in the more technical literature on the subject. This use has contributed to the suspicion with which the concept is often viewed. Mainly due to the influence of Marxist political and social theorists, the word 'ideology' is used to denote a theory which seeks to explain the origins and growth of *any* belief system by relating them to particular historical situations. Some writers in this tradition have argued that not only beliefs but also all kinds of knowledge are relative to particular social, economic and political situations, reflecting the interests and preferences of particular social groups. This theory continues to have its advocates especially within the popular theory of the 'sociology of knowledge'. However, many of its claims have been shown to be exaggerated and misleading, particularly as they refer to knowledge which satisfies universal or at least very general standards of truth (see chapter 3, and, for a fuller discussion, Lawton 1975). There are other ways of criticising ideologies than claiming a superior knowledge and disclosing the latent interests behind what institutions and people do and say. For example, some types of belief are subject to various processes of verification and they may be assessed according to the procedures of science and rational inquiry – they are not just a matter of personal preference. Other beliefs are more difficult to assess since they may form the core of an ideology, its foundation as it were upon which a whole structure of other beliefs, of values and of action commitments is erected. These beliefs are like declarations of faith and commitment and provide those who hold them with ways of looking at the world and talking about and acting within them, which are logically and psychologically prior to particular, testable statements within the ideology.

However, it is possible to look for *justifications* of belief statements and of value judgements within ideologies. It is a proper educational goal for a teacher to help a learner to become better able to assess his own value judgements and beliefs, as well as those of people subscribing to different ideologies in his society and other societies. Through a process of critical reflection and inquiry, pupils are able to develop the capacity substantially to modify their own ideologies, even rejecting those within which they are brought up and adopting new ones. In view of the power of ideology and its pervasiveness in life, it is strange that schools do not provide more opportunities to pupils to engage in ideological analysis and, on a wider plane, in cultural reflection and reinterpretation. There are dangers in this approach and some would argue that it is better for people to be less self-aware, less socially conscious, less deliberative and prescriptive in their thinking. Culture, it is sometimes said, is better when absorbed and assimilated unconsciously; it need not and ought not to become militant, prescriptive, systematic and action-orientated – i.e. ideological. But it is noteworthy that those who advocate this usually reserve to a small, elite group full powers of reflective self-consciousness and that, within *their* ideology, the mass of the population has a designated role to perform.

We shall conclude this chapter by considering two examples of ideological thinking in education. The first example comes from revolutionary mainland China, and consists of a draft programme, for primary and middle school education, published in 1969 in *The People's Daily* (reprinted in *Education in China*; London, Anglo-Chinese Educational Institute, 1974). It is difficult to know how far this and similar programmes have been implemented. Nevertheless, there are important insights to be gained into the ideological conception of education in a contemporary communist society, from reports of this nature.

According to the programme, *first*, schooling is to become subservient to politics, as interpreted by the poor and lower middle peasants who will lead the movement for educational reform. This intention tells us something about the ideological approach to education: *who* exercises power and authority is an important consideration; ideas about what is fitting and appropriate in education can change dramatically as changes occur in the distribution and balance of power in society.

Second, education is to be combined with 'productive labour', an ideal which is reflected not only in the content of the curriculum but also in the requirement that all office and brain workers, teachers included, are expected to undertake annually a period of manual labour.

Third, education is conceived as a total development process, concerning itself with moral, physical and intellectual well-being but within and in the furtherance of 'socialist consciousness and culture', of which Chairman Mao Tse-tung is the epitome and figurehead.

Fourth, education is to become merged with indoctrination, in that schools have the task of inculcating Chairman Mao's theory of 'continuing the revolution under the dictatorship of the proletariat'. There is no conception of a clash of ideas and theories in the Western liberal sense, or of encouraging learners to adjudicate amongst ideas, making up their own minds. However, as was noted previously, one ought not to assume too readily that the liberal educational ideal is free of political overtones – that it is ideologically free or neutral while only 'noisy' theories like those of communist education are ideologically laden.

Fifth, education in schools is to be linked to the life of the whole society through the active involvement in schooling of Communist Youth League members, Red Guards, parents and others.

Sixth, the traditional, dichotomised, institutional structures of schooling are to be dissolved and replaced by a common, nine-year school where preference shall be given to the children of 'workers, poor and lower middle peasants, revolutionary martyrs and armymen' and to those who excel politically and ideologically.

Lest it be supposed that a militantly ideological approach to education is, in our time, peculiar to countries like China, there are relationships to be explored, for example, between the curriculum of high status educational institutions in Europe – the selective secondary schools and the universities – and the ultimate social and economic status of those who pass through them. In a country like Britain, great emphasis is given to the national language, and to British history; teachers are trained to communicate a liberal ideology which is itself part of the cultural fabric, and the whole apparatus of schooling expresses and communicates certain kinds of values whilst excluding others. There is nothing odd or reprehensible about this. Our point here is simply that it would be a mistake to condemn education elsewhere for being 'ideological' whilst failing to recognize the ideological character of our own schooling.

Politics and education interrelate in a number of ways, not only through the overt uses of education by politicians to achieve political ends. The Chinese illustrations were intended to show that education is not merely a *means* to some political *end*. Education in itself seems to have a political dimension, and educational decision taking is seen as part of the political process. In our society, it is likely that the actual curriculum will be seen increasingly as an arena for action by pressure groups. Teachers will gain from learning how pressure groups work and – a more difficult but a more crucial lesson – learning how educational decisions express and reflect the values of a culture. The more teachers strive to make the curriculum 'socially relevant', 'practical', 'contemporary' and 'forward looking', the more do they invite political and public interest, at least in the policy aspects of their work.

A final example of the 'ideologising' of education will be taken from an area of the curriculum usually treated as a purely technical, non-political matter, namely the teaching of basic literacy. However, literacy has become a very 'hot' educational issue. Some of the *Black Paper* writers, for example, have expressed their concern over the tendency, as they see it, to replace basic literacy teaching in our schools with non-directive projects and even with subject matter of a political kind. Although nothing may be said quite as explicitly as this, it is not difficult to read into some of their arguments a claim that progressive and experimental practices are 'left wing' and 'socialist' while a traditional disciplined approach to reading instruction is not in any sense a political matter but simply a way of equipping future citizens to take their proper part in any kind of society. This claim would be more impressive if it were not for the plainly political bias in the *Black Paper* attacks on practices they don't like. However, the whole argument is likely to be sterile and inconclusive so long as we think only of the technical processes of reading instruction and ignore both the *content* of material presented for reading and the *context* of teaching and learning.

In our final illustration in this chapter, we shall consider briefly the ideas of one of the most challenging of contemporary educational theorists, the Brazilian Paulo Freire. As Freire's work with backward Latin American peasants has shown, many interesting and significant social and political issues are raised by decisions about *what* to teach adult farmers and farmworkers and *how* they are confronted with the challenge to learn.

Freire, like adult educators in a number of other developing societies, regards adult literacy as not only a matter of teaching grown ups *how* to read and write. The achievement of literacy is a key to cultural emancipation and to social change, and a liberation of the self from limited perceptions. The individual and social aspects of this process are united in the achievement of what Freire calls 'critical consciousness' (Freire 1973). This consciousness starts to emerge from encounters, through language, with the facts and events of everyday life, presented visually and orally in small discussion groups. Freire emphasises knowledge for use. But the use he has in mind is not that which produces form fillers and readers of the popular press – i.e. a combination of practical utility and rudimentary informational and leisure interests within a politico-social structure which remains untouched by these users. Rather, the use he has in mind is the capacity and willingness to work for a changed environment and community. Language is 'a force to transform the world'. Though Freire's theory is presented in heavy Marxist language, it emphasises processes which are familiar to teachers in the English, European and American progressive tradtions: creativity, subjectivity, self-awareness, and shared experience. But the progressive traditions in advanced western societies assume a literate culture and liberal values: educational processes are very often intended to induct and confirm, not to transform.

In Freire's literacy programme, words are units in a dialogue, in which status differences between teachers and taught are diminished. The symbolic group *circle* is used to emphasise the absence of hierarchy and control and the flow of ideas amongst members. The circle is termed a 'culture circle' and this refers both to the shared culture of its members and their determination to modify and possibly remake culture through learning. Words are selected as counters in the literacy process for their cultural significance, because they disclose what Freire terms 'dimensions of reality', which peasants brought up in a superstitious, impoverished environment are likely to accept as 'fate'. These are the 'generative words' on which not only a language course but also a culture regeneration programme might be built – words like 'slum', 'work', 'swampland'.

Freire is concerned particularly about how peasants *perceive,* and he encourages them to think critically and not passively about the society in which the objects and relationships they do perceive are to be found. Thus does literacy become part of an ideological programme which is open-ended, creative, critical, the consequence of dialogue and not of prescription or imposed authority. At least, this was his objective. In practice, it appears, not only did Freire meet opposition from the regime whose power he was challenging; even the peasants he was educating tended to stop short of the fullest development of 'critical consciousness' and to fall into more rigid, predefined positions.

Our reason for quoting Freire's work is to draw attention to two things which are often assumed but ought to be queried. First, that the technical processes of learning are content and value free and may be developed regardless of subject matter. Second, that the perceptions and values of learners make only an insignificant difference to their reception of topics, themes, subject matter and teaching situations. Furthermore, we want to stress a point which many curriculum theorists neglect entirely, that the design of the curriculum and the teaching of subject matter in schools are themselves forms of cultural action: curriculum making is a kind of cultural project (see chapters 2 and 5 for further development of this point).

Cultural projects involve both the school and the community. As we saw above, it is of vital importance to establish who has powers, rights and duties in relation to educational decisions. We should have greater cause to be concerned about the dangers of bias, partiality and indoctrination if curriculum decisions were to be left entirely to individual teachers. One way of overcoming these dangers is to involve more socially representative groups, including parents and pupils themselves, in the processes of curriculum decision taking. This raises the problem of distinguishing between professional and lay responsibility, but we cannot solve this problem by pretending that individual teachers or even teachers as a profession have a monopoly of the knowledge, expertise and social authority that are relevant to curriculum making.

The conception of the curriculum as a cultural project raises other difficulties which need to be resolved. Two kinds of curriculum and teaching strategies may be distinguished: those which equip students with the means to interpret, assess, and redefine what they are being taught, and those which promote acquiescence and passive acceptance. As noted above, these are not equivalent, respectively, to non-ideological and ideological approaches, but the former does attempt to meet some of the objections to ideological 'noise' (that it leads to indoctrination and manipulation). It is within the power and should be part of the responsibility of the teacher to encourage pupils to be more reflective, critical and analytic. When education is linked to programmes of national development and cultural renewal, there need not be – although in practice there often is – a conflict between creative and critical thinking, and the processes of cultural reconstruction. Perhaps the best example of a practical attempt to harmonize the two is to be found in President Nyerere's conception of 'education for self-reliance' within the Tanzanian socialist state (Nyerere 1973, and Open University 1975).

Whatever may be appropriate in single party, monolothic, or totalitarian societies, in pluralistic societies where there is the possibility of fundamental differences of value and beliefs within the law and where there exist long-standing institutions designed to foster and support diversity and variety, and where freedom is taken to include the rights of individuals not to conform to a uniform creed, schools have tasks other than those of promoting the interests and viewpoints of particular groups. We might put this more precisely by saying that schools have a duty to maintain openness of outlook and variety of value and belief.

Summary

The concept of ideology is valuable in curriculum thinking in alerting us to the way in which interest groups articulate implicit values and beliefs into coherent systems of ideas and action. These may be used either to oppose or to support cultural trends. Ideological analysis is therefore a key element in curriculum analysis. Ideologies of culture have a powerful effect in mobilising thought and feeling, and sustaining curriculum action. Moreover, an ideology of culture can take the form of a system of procedural values: consistent recourse to creative enquiry, social accountability and reconstruction in curriculum. The position adopted in this book, sometimes known as cultural reconstructionism, and owing much to the philosopher John Dewey, is an attempt to articulate such an ideology.

Further reading

It is important to read at least one of the three books by Freire listed in the bibliography at the end of the book. Corbett (1965) is an accessible and readable book which relates the concept of ideology to the wider arena of moral and social debate.

8 THE CULTURAL INTERPRETATION OF CURRICULUM DECISIONS

In themselves the concepts for the analysis of curriculum as culture discussed in chapters 3 to 7 (social structure and function; symbolic forms and systems; beliefs and values; ideology) tell us nothing about the world of day-to-day curriculum pressures and decisions. Indeed, such general concepts can be used to explain away puzzling or discordant aspects of curriculum experience by providing convenient labels for them ('It's our ideology', 'It was functional to use this syllabus', etc). If such concepts are to be used honestly and penetratively, more thought must be given to how abstract ideas of this kind can really be applied to concrete expressions of culture in idiosyncratic curriculum situations.

The need for these 'arts' of cultural interpretation can be illustrated through two instances of cultural *mis*interpretation. The first example arose at a conference on teaching about the Third World. A contributor made the valid point that to think of such countries as 'underdeveloped' was to undervalue their existing culture. It tended to assume that our technologically advanced culture was superior, that standards of living were the main criterion of development. He went on to argue that we ought to point out to children the irrational beliefs and prejudices that our colonial past and social structure have bequeathed us in the form, for example, of racist jokes and mythologies. But this is to interpret the symbolic function of jokes and myths much too literally. Consider this joke from the American South: the Romans cast an unarmed African slave into the arena of the Colosseum, together with a lion. After an exhausting struggle he killed it by biting through its throat. The Roman emperor would not spare the slave's life. 'Just like a negro,' he observed, 'they never fight fair.' Forms of expression of this kind provide far too revealing a window into our consciousness to be censored as irrational.

The second example of cultural misinterpretation is the misuse of Bernstein's early theorising about the relationship between class structure and symbolic forms (Bernstein 1965), and his distinction between 'elaborated' and 'restricted' codes of language. His ideas were sometimes used to reinforce middle class beliefs about the intrinsic limitations of working class language (Rosen 1972; Keddie 1973). But a major reason for the misinterpretations of working class children's verbal responses to classroom questioning may be that teachers tend to perceive them in terms of what they lack: the grammatical and semantic conventions which middle class culture enshrines. Teachers may be unaware of the unfamiliarity of the roles imposed upon working class children when they are asked artificial questions in school settings. Classroom questions and assignments are nearly always highly stylised, and presuppose the adoption of a particular role on the child's part. How often in working class culture do children have to explain something to someone who already knows the answer? In order to give 'successful' answers he has to take over the teacher's frame of reference, and be able to guess what sort of an answer the teacher expects. But because the working class child's out-of-school reality is often so different from that of a middle class teacher, the child generally fails to do this, while the teacher usually tends to brush aside his hesitant response in the flow of the classroom situation.

An old teaching anecdote illustrates the effect of incongruent frames of reference. An inspector visited a village school in a rural area. He pinned up a picture of a sheep and asked the class what it was. Nobody could answer. He quickly passed on, but later took a child aside and asked why nobody had been able to answer the question. 'Well, Sir,' said the child, 'we couldn't tell whether it was a pure Cheviot or a crossbreed.'

But our main concern in this chapter is to interpret curriculum decisions themselves as cultural phenomena without oversimplifying their practical character. Any teacher makes a stream of decisions to adjust the relationship between his or her time and energy; the ways in which knowledge and skills are created and developed in others; school resources and management; and the expectations of children, parents and society at large. Some of these decisions are made so rapidly and intuitively as hardly to count as decisions. At all stages in their work teachers make overall judgements of great complexity. But these judgements derive from and impinge upon more explicit and carefully considered plans and value systems. We can try to crystallise the all-important interplay between these plans and values and ongoing school pressures.

A concrete example will help here. The diagram in Figure 8.1 is a simplified attempt to conceptualise the stream of a primary school teacher's thought and decisions in using and then abandoning an educational television series on the theme 'Communication'. It illustrates the interweaving of 'practical' and ideological influences, and the difficulty of separating them. Much more could be said about the context than there is space to spell out here; but here is a cultural interpretation, albeit in compressed, perhaps provocative form.

Like many primary school teachers, the teacher had assimilated while at college a view of education which stresses the teacher's creative role in the nurturing of children's capacities: his duty to 'discover', 'follow' and

Aspects of teacher's experience which discouraged use of programmes	Aspects of teacher's experience which encouraged use of programmes

First Viewing

Booklet on programmes suggested that the subject matter was relevant to teachers' curriculum aims

But language of programmes seemed difficult

Children show great interest in material

Second Viewing

Confusing information in programme

Children write freely in follow-up lesson

No stimulus for art and craft work

Third Viewing

Materials seemed too hard for age-group

Follow-up suggested in booklet bored children

Fourth Viewing

Programme contained ideas on language as codes with which teacher was unfamiliar

Clear explanations of ideas in booklet.

Considerable interest in idea of codes and creative response (e.g. invention of own symbols) from brighter pupils

Reminder to teacher by headmaster that it was teacher's turn to mount school display

Teacher's concern at lack of ready material and recall of previous successful display on traditional theme ('Transport through the Ages')

Decision to give up Communications and concentrate on display topic

8.1 *A Sequence of Curriculum Decisions*

90

'nourish' the developing interests of the individual child. His guiding image of 'good' classroom activity was one of children pursuing minimally directed projects with strong, expressive elements, rather than carefully sequenced intellectualised assignments. Yet the variations in his sense of satisfaction in what his class was doing reflected the impact of other cultural influences. Both his headmaster and local authority adviser had recently emphasised the need for the more systematic promotion of basic skills of literacy and numeracy, so he was disposed to use externally devised resources which might give him more time to monitor children's progress. Moreover, it is seldom possible to detach curriculum decisions from teachers' attitudes to authority and the legitimacy of the pressures it brings. The relations between teachers and headmaster in that school were formal, and the teacher was uncomfortably aware of how the head evaluated the work of his class. In that sense, it was the social relations of the school that influenced his decision to discontinue an intellectually challenging but risk-laden experience. And not, as he might claim, his appraisal of children's needs, whether derived from psychological concepts or educational theory.

But the teacher in question felt that this interpretation was not quite right. He saw his decisions more in terms of a response to practical pressures of time and energy. He agreed that in his early years of teaching he had been strongly influenced by a romantic child-centred ideology, but said that he drew upon it now because it seemed to work, and because its language provided a convenient shorthand for justifying what he was doing to advisers and people like the authors of this book. He did not feel that he was unduly deferential to his head's authority and likely evaluation of his display; rather, he thought that it was prudent to appear to be so.

Nevertheless, our analysis was suggestive of the cultural influences and conflicts that all teachers experience. It serves to articulate the interplay between the concepts and belief

91

systems with which teachers think, the social relations of the school, and the daily round of classroom problems. It indicates how culture or, rather, cultural processes structure the teachers' perception of curriculum situations. Culture sets the stage upon which individual teachers make continuous valuations of what is possible. In becoming conscious of their role as mediators of culture, they may become aware of alternative stage settings.

A further point needs to be made about the cultural interpretation of a teacher's curriculum decisions. Its value depends on the extent to which it can be communicated to and criticised by the teachers themselves. It does not matter that teachers do not agree completely with the interpretation, nor that it is impossible to prove that it is true in an 'objective' or 'scientific' sense. What matters is that they can appraise the interpretation and comment to the effect that: 'It was something like that, though I didn't think of it in that way at the time. For instance, . . .'

Many frustrating problems of curriculum change result from the absence of a *milieu* of analysis and discussion. Symptoms of this neglect are that teachers feel that they have little choice in what they can do, because they feel enmeshed in webs of organisational constraints, other people's expectations and limited resources of time, money and materials. The case study material that follows suggests how such a situation may reflect a lack of integration in the culture of a school. There may be unacknowledged gaps between the ideology and concepts of curriculum advanced for a school, the conceptions, beliefs and skills of its staff, and its social conventions and processes. The case study concerns the effect of the 'open plan' conception within a particular school; but it has implications in the much wider debate about how curriculum change ought to be planned.

The hopes of an education authority which has introduced open plan approaches in a number of schools have been summarised as follows:

(1) The children come into contact with more teachers and other adults. They are able to take advantage of a teacher's special interests, enthusiasms, and expertise. They are able to talk to adults in a much freer manner . . . and their language development benefits accordingly.

(2) The individual child gains in self-confidence, not only through his expanded relationship with adults, but also because of his wider contacts with his peers. Although he is largely responsible for his own work, . . . he has to learn to work harmoniously with a number of other children. . .

(3) By cutting down the amount of circulation space required, the open-plan school should offer more teaching space . . . should give flexibility to the curriculum . . .

(4) Education in the open-plan school demands an essentially child-centred approach . . . The child is gaining in skill using resources and developing powers of initiative . . . but in a situation which must be highly structured by the teacher.

(5) Open-plan schools demand much work on the part of the teaching staff. . . The functions of individual spaces have to be allocated and sometimes timetabled. . . Standards of work should be higher than those attained in cellular schools if open-plan design is to be fully justified.

Since the public enquiry into the William Tyndale Junior School, Islington, discussion of the implementation of open plan approaches by particular schools has become a touchy issue. The material below refers neither to a school in that area, nor to one in the area of the education authority whose letter is quoted. The school now has some 240 pupils aged seven to eleven years. It was purpose built as an open plan school to replace an old building with traditional classroom design. The headmaster had the initially fully open teaching space compartmentalised bays separated by partitions. The school has eight full-time teachers each responsible for a subject area as follows: English (two), maths (two), art/craft (two), environmental studies (two). Each teacher has an area, called a home bay, where he takes a group of thirty children for registration. No teacher sees his register group all together except at registration.

After the system had been working for nearly a year an outside observer prepared a case study, of which the following is a part.

(1) All the eight teachers said that the open plan system had brought them extra stress; but that there had not been any deterioration in pupils' work.

(2) They felt that the open design had brought additional noise and distracting movement; but the partitioning had prevented the team-teaching and flexibility that might have offset it.

(3) The keeping of pupils' records and the planning of activities had become crucially important; yet, because of the increased problem of pupil control, work was more difficult to monitor.

(4) None of the staff considered that the school was really functioning on the open plan model. They were very conscious of the head's constant vigilance against any departure from the orderliness associated with traditional cellular methods.

(5) Four of the eight felt that many of the children were gaining in social and independent learning skills. They felt that quiet, shy children needed more attention than before.

(6) The teachers maintained that they were open-minded about the open-plan system, though their training had

been traditional and they had received no preparation for the new system. Parents had been fully informed of the system, but not consulted.

(7) There were no plans for modification of the system at that time.

Our presentation of the observer's report is of necessity selective. In effect the reader is being asked to make a third-hand cultural interpretation of curriculum decisions. The first interpretation was that of the observer; the second was our interpretation in choosing parts of his interpretation, for the original case study was fuller and was one of a number of similar studies (in half of which the open plan system was working relatively smoothly). Moreover, it must be emphasised that the material presented in no way justifies criticism of the open plan conception itself, or of the headmaster and other staff involved. Curriculum changes of this scale may take several years to establish. By seeing curriculum in terms of cultural interpretation, a teacher can avoid attributing curriculum problems to the shortcomings of particular ideas or particular individuals. Rather, it is to look at a complex situation, acknowledging its circumstantiality, but trying to discern the interplay between the symbolic forms available (for example, the open plan conception and the wider system of ideas about open education), the particular social processes amongst the people concerned, and their belief and value systems.

Guided by this frame of reference, we can focus on, for example, the effect of particular symbolic acts or forms, or the absence of shared values and conceptions of problems. The changed function of registration is a minor but telling instance. The form that registration takes in conventionally planned primary schools combines normative force and organisational effectiveness. It serves as a symbol of the teacher's authority on behalf of the community, and of the unity and continuity of the learning group. It is a ritual which anchors the ebb and flow of the child's experience. It also enables the teacher to survey the overall pattern of children's attendance and progress, and to follow up individual problems without disrupting his teaching. But if the teacher's relationship with the children on the register becomes administrative and pastoral only, all of these culturing processes may be weakened.

This is not to argue that the system of registration developed in cellular classrooms must be preserved (as noted in chapter 3, the weakness of the functional approach is that it is inherently conservative). But it is to stress two points. First, there are subtle interdependencies in school life which need analysis *before* large-scale changes are undertaken. Secondly, it is inevitable that when such changes are implemented, they will expose issues of values and personal relationships which are too frequently glossed over in the initial planning.

We can look at the broader aims of open plan design in a similar way. It is one thing to accept a statement of educational aims and values, such as that formulated by the education authority. It is another thing to consider what detailed action and decisions it involves, what changes in roles, relationships and styles of teaching will result. It seems clear that the open plan conception had only limited meaning for both headteacher and staff; and that their willingness to 'give the idea a fair chance' was inadequate preparation for its implementation. Inevitably it brought out the incongruence between the local authority's anxiety not to impose the change, the head's determination to preserve traditional 'standards', and the conceptions of curriculum planning that the teachers had built up in a different organisational framework. In any case, could they be expected to make the open plan system work when the head's implicit beliefs and actions contradicted the declared aims?

To recognise the difficulty of coordinating infinitely varied curriculum decisions made by different people over lengthy periods of change is to recognise the crucial role of the flow and articulation of ideas amongst teachers. If the means for it are not available, the most detailed plans of aims, objectives and procedures will do little to promote common interpretations of ideas and emphases in teaching. In the case of open plan schools, the aims entail such a long and complex chain of actions that the key problems in implementing the aims cannot all be anticipated. Provision must be made for early recognition of unforeseen difficulties, and for continually adapting and reinterpreting both ends and means.

But for this to happen there must be provision for the honest exploration and evaluation of what is intended, what is acutally happening, and what is feasible. This has to involve parents and children as well as teachers if statements of aim or ideology are not to lead to the concealment of difficulties and disagreements. It does *not* follow that radical curriculum change can proceed only on the basis of complete agreement and consensus about change; or on the basis of comprehensive prior research into likely effects; or with the optimistic expectation that a harmonious integration of ideas, value systems and social processes can be maintained. But it does follow that teachers and others concerned with intitiating and implementing such changes should interpret them in the context of culture; and should be able to recognise and justify the cultural implications of their actions.

As we noted at the end of our earlier example of cultural interpretation, culture sets the stage upon which individual teachers make valuations of what is possible. The open plan conception is an attempt to bring about cultural development by creating new stage settings in both a physical and symbolic sense. But new stage settings demand new roles and new skills, which take time to build up. The neglected problems of curriculum are those of how schools can progressively reinterpret older roles and skills.

Summary

The curriculum culture of particular schools or teachers cannot be fully explained in terms of social control, symbolic systems and value systems. Each situation presents an individual problem of cultural interpretation, each requiring tentative conjecture about how far generalisations about social forces, etc., do or do not illuminate particular beliefs and decisions. Skills of cultural interpretation and diagnosis are essential to effective communication about curriculum.

Further reading

It is significant how little has been written which effectively relates general sociological and curriculum concepts to complex particular cases. Richardson (1975) and Hargreaves (1973) are helpful here; so is Shipman (1974).

SCHOOLS AND THE CURRICULUM DESIGN PROCESS

The tasks of culture analysis and interpretation that have been discussed pose many problems in curriculum design and development for schools and the teaching profession. But in saying this we are not suggesting that only schools and teachers have a responsibility in curriculum design and development. Indeed the range of groups, agencies and institutions with a justifiable interest in curriculum is greater than is frequently realised even by teachers themselves. In general, educators have only become fully aware of the roles of the various contributors to curriculum decisions, and the different constraints, since curriculum development emerged as a distinctive facet of education in the 1950s and 1960s. In this chapter our aim is to consider specifically the role of the teacher and the concept of school-based curriculum development in the context of culture.

Labels in education can easily mislead. School-based curriculum development is a new name for an old idea. The idea crops up at all periods of educational history, in one guise or another. The basis of the idea is that the best place for designing the curriculum is where the teacher and learner meet. The Athenian philosophers of the Socratic school were spontaneous curriculum designers who built up their curricula, progressively, through dialogue. The starting point might be a question, a puzzle, the report of a view held by another philosopher in some distant place, or a conversation about current political and social issues. Thus the public places of Athens served as a school and the joint dialectical experiences of the teacher, his peers and his pupils constituted the curriculum. When assessing criticisms that are frequently made of modern progressive education, it is worth remembering that this informal, problem solving, project-like, interdisciplinary, non-bookish approach to learning characterised one of the most brilliant periods in intellectual history. But our point is less to draw attention to the antiquity of an idea, than to show that 'school-based curriculum development' is an *idea,* not simply a technique or an organisation device.

We suggested that a fruitful way of approaching the curriculum is to think of it as a mediation or a bridge between the learner's experiences and the processes, forms and substance of contemporary culture. To be defensible educationally, the curriculum must comprise mediating experiences which are meaningful to the learner and significantly broadening, stimulating, and guiding of his further growth. But, from the learner's point of view, the reality of school experience seldom measures up to this.

In secondary education particularly, the curriculum often consists of graded exercises of content mastery within the subject disciplines. More recently, these have been challenged and alternative 'child-centred' and 'socially relevant' schemes suggested. But neither the traditional curriculum nor these alternatives give a satisfactory account of the school's role as a culture mediator. The principal modes of experience, symbolic systems, patterns of meaning and forms of action which, as we argued in chapter 4, constitute culture, are not reducible either to 'subjects' as they are commonly taught for examination purposes, or to the partial, limited experiences and interests of pupils growing up.

Nevertheless, pupil experience and interests provide one of the fundamental foundations of the curriculum, and it is pointless to prepare syllabuses which do not incorporate some analysis of this experience. Thus the teacher needs sufficient freedom and skill in curriculum making to be able to build new learning experience on the basis of existing pupil learning. It can be said that this is simply part of what is meant by 'teaching'. When working within externally devised syllabuses, for example, teachers have to bring about some kind of mesh between pupils' interest and present level of understanding, and the topics and tasks of the syllabus. This is true, but it is a restrictive situation which contributes to many false assumptions about 'eliciting interests', 'motivation' and 'standards'. For example, children may tend to respond to teachers' interest in question-spotting and disparage what is not testable.

These considerations have led many teachers to think of alternative approaches to conventional subject teaching through school-designed curricula. Various kinds of (externally moderated) assessments can be built into such school-designed curricula. There is a steady – and in some countries quite dramatic – move in this direction, coupled with growing pupil dissatisfaction with conventional curricula. All this suggests that teachers will need more expertise in developing curricula and will not be able to depend either on externally devised syllabuses or on their own training in particular academic disciplines. Secondary teachers have much to learn here from their counterparts in primary schools.

If teachers are to enter fully into the planning of curricula, into the development of maps of culture and experience, they need both freedom and resources. As things stand at present, even the most understanding and knowledgeable teachers lack time, techniques and incentive to undertake thorough reviews of the individual and corporate needs of the pupils they teach. 'Needs' cannot be identified unless teachers commit themselves to value judgements and assessments of the longer-term development of their pupils. Though the diversity of pupil experience and the problems of linking that experience with wider aspects of culture are puzzling, they are not insurmountable, as we have shown in previous chapters. Making such judgements, being prepared to justify them, and looking into the future growth possibilities of pupils are tasks which members of the teaching profession have to take more seriously, if the locus of curriculum decision taking continues to shift from external and central agencies to the school itself. The school itself is surely the place where curricula which attempt this mediating task should be designed. We are not here considering alternatives to the contribution to be made by external agencies, such as teachers' centres, tertiary institutions, the inspectorate, text-book publishers, curriculum developments teams, etc. Clearly a network of supporting and cooperating agencies will be involved in any effective strategy of school-based curriculum development (see Adams 1975 for a fuller discussion of the supporting network of agencies and institutions). But our focus is on the case for school-based curriculum development and its central characteristics.

The school is not only the place where pupils of diverse interests, backgrounds, experiences, expectations and needs congregate. It is a social institution, a place in which educational experiences may occur naturally and comfortably, although not without great effort on the part of teachers and learners alike. The school may be thought of as an institution engaged in complex transactions with its environment, which involve exchanges of ideas, resources, and people through an elaborate, criss-crossing network of communications systems. That is, the school has a culture and schooling itself is one of the key cultural processes in modern society. Through these communications, between 'school' and 'world', understandings emerge, interpretations are made and meanings are acquired. In short, the school in its transactions with the world becomes a nodule of meaning with its own cultural features. We may think of school cul-

102

ture as, in part, an educational culture which shares many, but not all, of the features of other cultural systems in our society. There is a very great danger that this cultural nodule, the school, will cocoon itself, relating itself to the world in such a way as to raise rather than lower barriers, to impede easy and frequent exchanges, and to build up purely internal and domestic rituals, belief systems and patterns of meaning. The school curriculum can very easily become a form of cultural inwardness, of indwelling for its acolytes, the teachers, and its neophytes, the pupils. In order to be open and responsive to the whole culture, the school needs freedom and resources to build up its own curricula in a flexible exchange system with its environment. Guided by teachers who are sensitive to contemporary movements in society and skilled in culture analysis, curriculum making will strengthen and intensify the system of transactions and exchanges.

The principal arguments favouring school-based curriculum development are the need to relate the processes of curriculum making to the experience of the learner, and the life of the school to changing social realities. Externally devised syllabuses, textbooks and examinations all have some part to play, but their influence needs to be drastically changed so that their value can be experienced. They all help – or may help – to define educational values and set certain standards. In the on-going debate about examinations it can easily be forgotten that the conceptions and knowledge of scholars and other experts are a vital element in any form of education and that examination boards and textbooks can provde a forum for their views. This point is well understood in France and other continental countries. But we need better means of communicating this knowledge and expertise than syllabuses prepared externally to satisfy examination board requirements. The formation of teachers, and in particular the intellectual stimulus which students ought to receive during their training, is another potent but neglected influence on curriculum making.

The case for school-based curriculum development does not rest only on arguments about meeting pupil needs, responding to social change, and finding the most appropriate ways of sustaining scholarly and expert standards and values in schooling. There has been a marked reaction against a form of social and educational control which locates power and influence in a few key centres and then develops communication, dissemination and control systems to ensure that all the elements in the total system, the schools, teachers and pupils, are functioning according to plan. These systems, usually referred to as centralised and bureaucratic, seem not to work effectively and efficiently once they get beyond a certain level of complexity. Radical critics refer to them as manipulative and condemn the way in which they appear to serve the interests of small social elites – the managerial classes, the political, business and bureaucratic elites – whilst treating education as a commodity to be processed according to predefined social policy goals.

We do not propose to enter this debate, but merely to point out that the control of educational provision from a small number of central power bases, and the distribution of knowledge and understanding through syllabuses, textbooks and learning packages prepared under the control of influence of those occupying these power bases, are themselves examples of practical cultural interpretation. They are heavily charged with ideological content, and resisted, increasingly, by arguments with strong ideological overtones. The battle for the control of key decision points in national curriculum making is ideological in character – different groups competing for power to mediate culture to the school population.

Although the ideological tone of the debate was never very sharp, the struggle to control the Schools Council when it was set up in Britain in the early 1960s illustrates the importance that various groups attach to the question of *who* controls the curriculum. It appeared to the teachers' unions and to the local authorities that the then Ministry of Education was about to assert power in the curriculum field by setting up its own study and development group to initiate policy inquiries and projects. What emerged from a behind-the-scenes set of skirmishes, confrontations and agreements was the Schools Council, which took care in its terms of reference to affirm that it was not a controlling but a supporting and facilitating body. School-based curriculum development became an article of faith, which the subsequent activity of the Council has not always translated into a doctrine of works:

> The objects . . . are to uphold and interpret the principle that each school should have the fullest possible measure of responsibility for its own work, with its own curriculum and teaching methods based on the needs of its own pupils and evolved by its own staff: and to seek, through cooperative study of common problems, to assist all who have individual or joint responsibilities for, or in connection with, the schools' curricula and examinations to coordinate their actions in harmony with this principle (Schools Council 1965, p. 34).

The above passage is a masterly piece of balanced, conciliating official prose which provides the necessary loopholes ('fullest possible', 'needs', 'seek', 'assist', etc.). Such an exercise in conciliation which at the same time indicated a very wide range of possible departures for the ensuing work of the Council was necessary, and it indicates the political seriousness of the issue concerning curriculum control.

The policy of the Schools Council – after ten years of support for curriculum development projects mainly in single subjects, and a small number of specialist working parties on topics such as examination reform, the middle years of schooling and whole curriculum – is moving decisively towards the support of regional and local initiatives. In one of its publications the Council has identified three types of projects:

> (i) 'complete' course materials for pupils and teachers, intended, broadly speaking, to be used in a certain order (Schools Mathematics Project, for example); (ii) materials as a resource from which teachers are expected to select those suitable for their own pupils (Humanities Curriculum Project, for example); (iii) exemplar materials or teachers' guides to which teachers are expected to add from other publications or their own resources (Mathematics for the Majority, for example). (Schools Council 1973, pp. 41-2)

The Council noted a distinct swing, in its own projects, away from the first towards the second and third of these two approaches.

This swing is of considerable interest. In its early years, the Council elected to construct a framework of projects but did not develop a strategy of implementation and diffusion. Some of the more interesting of the projects, such as Humanities Curriculum Project, Mathematics for the Majority Continuation Project, and Science 5-13, provided plenty of scope for teacher contribution and invited teachers, either directly or indirectly, to choose from or supplement project materials. The Council itself, in the early 1970s, began to think much more seriously about applications, extensions and uses of its early project materials. But, of course, in making their selections, additions and extensions, teachers will construct their own interpretative frameworks, presenting to their pupils pictures of reality (as in the sciences, etc.), a selection of themes, issues, problems and possibilities for action (as in social studies, humanities, etc.), and frameworks for judging, assessing and acting. All of these teacher actions, at school and classroom level, are cultural interpretations.

To emphasise this point is to expose one of the difficulties about school-based curriculum development. It is the passivity of many teachers when challenged to undertake substantial responsibility for curriculum decisions. The very opportunity presented to teachers in school-based curriculum development is also a potential threat. Teacher self-actualisation and professionalisation become more of a possibility when freedom to develop curricula is increased. Teacher involvement in the processes of curriculum making is more consistent with a professional self-image, with a sense of professional achievement and the motivations underlying that achievement, and with a complex sense of personal worth than is the functionary image. Yet some studies of teacher motivation and interest in curriculum-making suggest that there is a significant proportion of teachers who prefer to play the more passive, functionary role.

The manner in which the teacher confronts the task of curriculum planning, which is an integral part of his teaching, tells us something about his picture of the world and how people should live in the world. This picture may be that of participatory action which is strong in individual responsibility, initiative and creativity, or it may be that of fitting into a bureaucratic scheme, strong in acquiescence and conformity. School-based curriculum development is in line with those movements in contemporary culture which give prominence to activism by small groups, the questioning of traditional hierarchies, and the substitution of the critical processes of inquiry and valuation for those of assimilation and value acceptance.

The active engagement of pupils, parents and other immediately interested parties is of no less importance in a comprehensive strategy of devolution of decision making. The operation of such a strategy will prove very difficult because the perceptions, values and expectations of each of the major parties will be different and there will be differences within them. As this movement gains momentum, we may expect value clashes as each group endeavours to extend the boundaries of its own world view.

Teachers, naturally, have expressed considerable anxiety over what they term 'parental interference'. In the light of our analysis, this term is misapplied since what the parents very properly recognise is that school life is of the utmost significance for their own children's experience and opportunities, and for social life as a whole. Hence the conflict is not primarily one of methods and procedures, or even of priorities for particular skills and subjects (early reading, mathematics instead of outdoor pursuits, etc.). Rather, it is based on a healthy recognition by parents that schools are, in fact, engaged in cultural projects. For this reason, teachers will need more skill and subtlety than hitherto. They will have to work with parents and pupils in the design of these cultural projects – that is, in curriculum design. They will not be able to maintain the pretence that they, the trained experts, know best.

While emphasising the part that has to be played by other groups and agencies, we want to focus on the leadership role that the teacher should be exercising in these wider involvements. How is the teacher to proceed in his task of curriculum making, given that he has a specialist role to perform and that other partners look to him for guidance in the processes of curriculum design? There is a fierce debate in curriculum development between advocates of technological planning models based on clear cut objectives and an assorted array of anti-technologists. The debate has taken the form of a miscellany of criticisms of and attacks on the managerial approach. They are followed by the presentation of a variety of alternatives, but they all are, strictly speaking, reactions to the management model which has become progressively more refined and simple. Its great attractions are its apparent ease of application, its conceptual simplicity and the use that has been made of it in curriculum design

Its weakness, essentially, is that its simplicity and practicality disguise conceptual problems and assumptions about the nature of teaching and learning processes which do not stand up to close analysis (see, for example, Stenhouse 1975, chapters 6 and 7).

Despite these deficiencies, there are features of the management model which *any* kind of curriculum development must take into account. If they are not linked as a series of tasks, as in the management model, they will have to be undertaken in some other way. Thus there is point in confronting the management model, exploring its possible uses, and, after assessing its worth, considering alternative ways of designing the curriculum.

The model can be summarised as a sequence of steps:

(1) Situational analysis
(2) Goal formulation
(3) Programme building
(4) Interpretation and implementation
(5) Monitoring, assessment, feedback reconstruction

In the remainder of this chapter we shall consider briefly what might be involved in each of the steps. But before we do this, the following points about the model should be noted:

(i) In the stricter technological form which it often takes, teachers are enjoined to follow the sequence. There is no necessity for this. The process can be entered at any one step.

(ii) Situational analysis is a step which does not usually feature in the management formulation; it is our belief that this is a crucial step, to which we shall give most attention.

(iii) The model makes no assumptions about the depth of exploration at any one stage; that is, how far practical constraints of time, resources, attitudes, can be changed or redefined.

(iv) The model does not assume that the task in education is to define a precise objective and to find the most effective and efficient means to attain that end.

Instead, its focus is experience. Through its use teachers can decide how they intend to modify experience: by setting up ends to pursue, providing material resources, confronting learners with assessments of their performances, and so forth.

Let us consider each of the five steps in the model, leaving situational analysis, the most significant process in the cultural approach to curriculum, until last.

Goal formulation: Goals statements need not refer to *ends* or *outcomes,* which are frequently beyond and outside the processes of learning and teaching. We may think of goals as culminations; for example, in carpentry, the finished chair is one goal for a particular part of a year's work. It is not the only goal (and perhaps not the most important since other goals will include pupil satisfaction, increased aesthetic sensibility, a growth in skills of various kinds, etc). It is part of a continuing process, not an end point (since better chairs and other, more demanding, objects can be made, and in making the chair the pupil should develop an interest in 'going on'). We may also think of goals as *qualitative* aspects of learning experience, which will manifest themselves progressively.

In short, the advice often given by technologists to teachers, to specify *all* their goals in advance, in terms of discrete items of measurable behaviour, is fatuous. Despite its claims to practical utility, it is quite impracticable. Some goals may be formulated in this way, but they refer only to a very small part of what is important in education.

Programme building: The selection of subject matter for learning, its arrangement into a sequence of teaching episodes, and the choice of appropriate supporting materials and media of presentation, is what we mean by programme building. There is, however, a tendency to regard it as 'non-teaching' time, rather than to treat it as an integral part of the teaching process. The preparation of lessons and learning materials provides opportunities for teachers to think out, in a concrete and systematic way, the cultural meanings and symbols which pupils will encounter in their learning. For example, curriculum content and teaching methods may present knowledge either as a finished product or as the outcome of continuing inquiry; they may either mask assumptions and blur distinctions or provoke critical appraisals.

These are polarisations intended to suggest that the programme building stage of the curriculum design process presents opportunities to consider the way in which learners will receive and respond to materials and methods which may be taken for granted by the teacher.

Are there any general criteria governing the choice of content and the design of learning activities? According to our analysis, there are several which we shall simply enumerate. Learning tasks should be:

(1) *Meaningful* to the learner – they must be such that he is able and ready to see their significance and value and to grasp their intelligibility.
(2) *Economical* in the sense that repetitiveness and redundancy are avoided, and the simplest and most powerful ways of acquiring knowledge, skills and understanding are followed.
(3) *Structured* into a pattern or system and not treated as discrete elements.
(4) *Inviting*, so that learners are stimulated to embark upon the hard work that will be entailed.
(5) *Activity-centred*, in the sense that they indicate ways in which the pupil himself will be actively engaged in processes of inquiry and creativity, even where routine tasks are part of the learning cycle.

111

This is not an exhaustive list but it forms the basis of the criteria against which content and learning activities should be judged.

Interpretation and implementation: The task in this phase of curriculum design is to anticipate the plan for the installation of the curriculum in the school or the classroom. Two kinds of task stand out: identifying difficulties and possible resistance, and planning the resources and the organisational changes that might be needed. In a design model it is important to anticipate difficulty rather than to trust to the experience and goodwill of others or one's own native wit and judgement. There is now a considerable literature on problems of implementing organisational and institutional change to which reference ought to be made in any piece of systematic curriculum planning which goes beyond lesson planning (see, for example, Hoyle 1972, Richardson 1975, and The Open University 1975).

Monitoring, assessment, feedback and reconstruction: A change in the curriculum has effects which go beyond the selection and teaching of new content. Thus it requires more comprehensive forms of evaluation than have been common in schools hitherto. Even the simplest exercise in curriculum design will incorporate a scheme of some sort for evaluating performance. What is inadequate is to confine this evaluation to an assessment of pupil learning. Wider tasks of evaluation include:

(1) Providing for on-going assessment which permits further changes in the objectives and programmes in the light of classroom experience.
(2) Assessing a wide range of outcomes, such as pupil attitudes, reactions of other teachers, and the impact of the curriculum changes on the school organisation as a whole.
(3) Keeping adequate records which are based on the

response of a variety of participants, not only those most directly involved in the change.

(4) Developing a range of assessment procedures appropriate to the outcomes which are being analysed.

Although it is something that infant school teachers have been doing for decades, we recognise that it is demanding for an individual teacher to engage systematically in curriculum development. A team approach to curriculum development is to be preferred. If school development teams are to work satisfactorily they need the support of school principals and of their colleagues; they need time and resources. But we have yet to discuss one stage in the model which is of particular importance in curriculum development conceived as cultural development.

Situational analysis: The concept of a *situation to be analysed* is central to the cultural approach we have adopted. Teaching and learning are processes in which exchanges and transformations occur – exchanges between teacher and learner, and transformation of the pupils' awareness and competence. But there is an initial state in which the learner finds himself, affected by many factors of which the teacher needs to be aware. This state and these factors are what we term the 'situation'. It is constituted of interacting elements all of which need to be taken into account in a comprehensive design for learning. *How* these elements are interpreted and *how* the teacher's attempts to account for this in his curriculum planning make important differences to the learning activities that ultimately take place in the classroom. These interpretations are part of what is meant by a cultural analysis of the curriculum.

The task of situational analysis may be approached through a review of (*a*) external and (*b*) internal factors. The distinction is not a hard and fast one but it enables us to focus on broader contextual issues on the one hand, and on the immediate school environment on the other. These are all factors about which in however limited and partial a manner, information is needed by teachers who are undertaking curriculum design:

(a) *External factors:*
　(1) Changes and trends in society which indicate tasks for schools – e.g. industrial development, political directives, cultural movements, ideological shifts.
　(2) Expectations and requirements of parents, employers.
　(3) Community assumptions and values including patterns of adult-child relations.
　(4) The changing nature of the subject disciplines.
　(5) The potential contribution of teacher support systems including teachers' centres, colleges of education and universities, etc.
　(6) Actual and anticipated flow of resources into the school.

(b) *Internal factors:*
　(1) Pupils, their aptitudes, abilities, attitudes, values and defined educational needs.
　(2) Teachers, their values, attitudes, skills, knowledge, experience and special strengths and weaknesses.
　(3) School ethos and political structures, common assumptions and expectations including traditions, power distribution, etc.
　(4) Material resources, including plant, equipment and learning materials.
　(5) Perceived and felt problems and shortcomings in existing curriculum.

This summary outline of factors to be examined can give only a schematic indication of the nature of the task of situational analysis. Many teachers make such analysis intuitively and rapidly. There is a place for an impressionistic approach but it has its dangers. With experience, teachers, like all practitioners, can become complacent and develop faulty habits. It is extremely difficult to get information on some elements in the scheme, and there is accordingly a temptation to skim over them, to ignore them altogether, or to take partial, one-sided views. Thus there are advantages, even for experienced teachers embarking on curriculum development, in working through the elements of a situational analysis in a systematic manner, and preferably in a group setting that involves outside advisers.

Summary

We have indicated the principal tasks to be undertaken in curriculum design. The way in which we have conceptualised and defined the process differs significantly from that of most previous writers in the field. You will need to consider whether this approach relates the need for a systematic, analytic strategy to the need to come to terms with practicalities of school life. But our emphasis has been on *processes* of designing and we have said very little about the substantive issues. What could a curriculum which sets out to orientate pupils towards the principal issues, trends and developments in contemporary culture look like ? In the next chapter, which is concerned with policy issues, we shall sketch the outlines of a culture core curriculum.

Further reading

See Jenkins and Raggatt (1974) for a further discussion of the situational approach to curriculum planning, and Stenhouse (1975) on the 'process model' of curriculum planning. For a discussion of the 'centralist' *v.* 'localist' approaches to curriculum development see Thompson and White (1975).

10 NATIONAL POLICY: A COMMON CORE CULTURAL CURRICULUM

In the previous chapter we discussed some of the arguments in favour of devolving greater responsibility for curriculum making upon schools and outlined a possible design model. Two questions were raised, which we shall now consider further. The first of these is the support structure needed to sustain school-based curriculum development, and the second is the outline of the content of a culture core curriculum. These two questions can be considered together inasmuch as one element in a support structure for school-based curriculum development is a broad framework of curriculum content within which individual variations and developments at the school level might be attempted. There are other aspects of a support system of an organisational kind, such as resource centres, teachers' centres, research institutes, teacher education programmes and so forth. However, we shall not be concerned so much with these as with the policy problem of defining a broad curriculum framework within which individual curricula might be developed.

But, first, what is a common core curriculum? Simply stated it is a set of common learning experiences which all pupils undergo; looked at more closely, few common core curricula are as 'common' as they appear at first glance. For example, it is a legal requirement in England and Wales that schools should provide a corporate morning act of worship and regular religious instruction. On the face of it, England and Wales would seem to have religious education as one element in a common curriculum. But the legal requirement is interpreted in such diverse ways – and not infrequently ignored – so that the reality of common religious education is very different.

Granting the diversity in practice of any common element in a nation's curriculum, it is still possible to lay out in broad outline a range of learning experiences to which all pupils in a school system are or might be exposed. In the British educational system and others like it, we have a rough approximation of a common core curriculum comprising the subjects of English, history, geography, mathematics, science, physical education and religious education. This basic framework is to be found in some form in most primary and secondary schools up to the fifth year. Thereafter, greater specialisation and diversification effectively break the common programme. In considering arguments *for* a common core curriculum, we should appreciate that we already have its rudiments.

On the other hand, the growing number of schemes based on projects, interdisciplinary studies, themes, topics and the variety of offerings now available within the conventional subjects suggests that the diversity of curriculum elements are as significant as the common elements. Indeed, it is not difficult to produce a powerful case for greater differentiation and individualisation of curricula. For example, a complete education for one pupil could be built upon a foundation in, say, language; for another, upon a foundation in sciences. Accepting that there are defensible alternatives (and that there are dangers if the idea is driven too hard, for example, of political manipulation from a powerful ministry), we feel that the case for a common core curriculum ought to be considered very seriously.

The most important reason for developing a common core curriculum derives from a thesis about culture itself, and the relationship of cultural experience to social life (see chapter 1). We have to ask ourselves whether there are values and experiences which it is desirable and necessary for all members of a society to share. What is meant by this is that the idea of a society presupposes some common or shared outlooks, providing the framework at least of a common culture. Building a sense of community means developing a common sense of values and providing for some common experiences. This emphasis on shared or common culture does not in any way limit individuality in the pursuit of specialist interests and minority concerns. Nor does the notion of a common culture, when defined in relation to a particular society, preclude the development of more universal interests and concerns. Thus the ideas of a European, American, African or Pacific community, and of world citizenship, remote as they may appear from everyday experience and present political realities, are not inconsistent with the pursuit of common national cultural experiences. Part of the task of developing a common core cultural curriculum is to work out various layers and levels of common and differentiated experience and relate particular curriculum choices to the different levels. For example, the historical dimension of a common core curriculum may refer to local, regional, national, and world levels of culture. All have their place at some stage in the child's development, but if a systematic approach is not adopted, one or another (usually local or national history) tends to predominate. Thus a cultural approach to the curriculum encourages a more comprehensive and thoroughgoing analysis of the level and type of cultural experience which is to be given prominence at any particular stage of schooling. This is not the kind of decision that ought to be taken at the local level, but should be worked out at the level of the whole system, providing a policy framework within which schools can make their own arrangements for their own individual pupils.

A core curriculum could be built partly around the experience, analysis and appraisal of these characteristics of particular cultures, both to develop greater awareness of cul-

118

tural heritages and to stimulate cultural criticism and reconstruction. The idea of cultural reconstruction is suspect to Professor Bantock and to the thinkers in the traditions of which he is a part, notably D. H. Lawrence and F. R. Leavis (Bantock 1968). They seem to prefer to leave to chance, to ill-defined psychic and social forces, those cultural processes of transmission, exchange, reappraisal and development which deeply affect the well-being of everyone. A rational and humanistic approach to the problems of continuity and growth of society and culture, when civilised values are constantly under threat from irrationalism, violence, economic fluctuation and exploitation, is to try to work out the kind of society we would like, to indicate so far as we are able principal cultural features, and to strive for their realisation.

Schools can be crucial agencies in this process. Thus a common core curriculum in schools may be thought of as a kind of map or chart of the experiences, thought processes and life styles that we regard as worthwhile. What is common about it is its generality, universality and communicability: it is capable of being shared, enjoyed and valued by all.

There are further considerations in favour of an attempt to build up a common core curriculum. Without some common elements in the curriculum, social and economic mobility within a population are difficult, if not impossible. Providing approximately equal opportunities for all means having some common elements, as does the maintenance of high standards overall for the educational system. Finally, education has universal characteristics, notably the quest for rationality, which are most easily expressed through the fundamental themes of thought, enquiry and action which provide part of the substructure of a common curriculum. To elaborate these points would require careful and detailed treatment well beyond the scope of this volume. Our principal point is that there are relationships between a common core curriculum and the pursuit of a common culture which a national educational policy must actively promote.

Unfortunately, the structures for curriculum development in Britain, as in many other countries, have been insufficiently used for these purposes. The Schools Council seems to be the one national agency that might have made a contribution to the cultural analysis we are proposing. It is semi-independent of government, representative of a reasonable spectrum of educational interests, and it has been commissioned in the most general way to promote and support curriculum development. The Council has not so far sponsored or stimulated wide-ranging culture analysis and has shown relatively little interest in the idea of a national framework for curriculum policy. Given the power struggle which took place when it was being set up and its apparent devotion to materials production and to strategies and techniques of innovation, evaluation, etc., it is doubtful whether much is to be expected of the Council at this time (consider, for example, the Schools Council Working Paper (1975) on *The Whole Curriculum*).

Clearly, the task of developing a national policy on a core curriculum, and the outlines of and, possibly, exemplary materials for the bases of such a curriculum, is a very substantial one indeed. But there is growing interest in drawing these outlines and in creating more coherent decision structures than we have at present (see White 1973 and Lawton 1975). A widening debate of the issues by thinkers and practitioners from a wide range of disciplines and walks of life is necessary if this movement is to become significant.

Teachers have an important part to play in this movement. First, they can contribute to developing school curricula which are focused on culture, its interpretation and development. Secondly, they can work to establish and support structures for the creation of national curriculum policy, preferably through semi-autonomous bodies like the Schools Council, and comparable bodies in other countries, where the possibility of political manipulation is reduced, and

120

independent views might be freely expressed.

What might a common cultural core curriculum look like? Some proposals have been made by curriculum theorists (those of Smith, Stanley and Shores 1957 were outlined in chapter 1; see also Broudy, Smith and Burnett 1966 and Lawton 1973). Each of these proposals is interesting and significant but none quite meets the requirements as we see them. Smith, Stanley and Shores played a pioneering role in American educational theory, but their ideas are now dated and over-related to the American situation of the 1950s. Broudy, Smith and Burnett's scheme is a penetrating analysis, but the curriculum framework they propose is too intellectualistic for a mass system of secondary education. Professor Lawton's outline is designed specifically for English education, but we are not convinced that it is grounded sufficiently in the concrete experiences of pupils as distinct from the disciplines of knowledge. In any case, our analysis of culture is sufficiently different from his for us to propose a somewhat different schematisation.

We accept that no general curriculum outline will be adequate if it overlooks the fundamental intellectual, emotional, historical and social significance of the forms and fields of knowledge. Much valuable work has been done in recent years in the analysis of these forms and fields (see, for example, Hirst and Peters (1970), Phenix (1964), Chanan and Gilchrist (1974), Skilbeck (1975); also the discussion in chapter 5 of the distinction between detached and involved modes of thought). But how knowledge is divided and classified for intellectual or any other uses is not entirely a matter of logic and epistemology. There are several ways in which the knowledge cake might be cut. Furthermore, the logical analysis of knowledge, as practised by Hirst, has yielded forms or disciplines which correspond closely to high status academic subjects. Thus some of his critics not unreasonably suggest that, despite his disclaimers, he is resurrecting the grammar school curriculum and offering it as a universal

121

curriculum design. This is not his stated intention, nor is it a necessary consequence of the kind of analysis he has made. However, we do not believe that it is possible to construct a common core curriculum for universal education directly upon the basis of the separate forms of knowledge, because of their incompleteness as a map of human culture and their strongly intellectualistic character.

Similarly, the attempts made by progressive educationists to build universal curricula upon the defined characteristics of the individual learner do not seem to us to meet the requirements of a cultural approach. In fact, no curriculum *can* be constructed upon defined characteristics of learners unless assumptions and choices are made about the *direction* which the development or enhancement of these characteristics of learners is to take. A clear framework of educational as distinct from unstructured and untutored growth is necessary. If this framework is not to consist of the traditional forms of knowledge, dressed up as interesting new subjects and projects, what might it look like?

Let us go back for a moment to our analysis of culture, when we drew attention to: (1) the systems of symbolic and expressive forms in language, art, myth and ritual, science, etc., which enable us to focus experience; (2) the processes of social interaction and control, which enable us to share and coordinate experience; and (3) the complexes of beliefs, values, customs, skills, etc., which further define and differentiate symbolic forms and social processes. These three constituents as components of culture may be construed as a kind of map or chart. The common core culture curriculum is concerned to identify fundamental, universal aspects of culture, and to introduce pupils to these aspects through specific, concrete expression and realisations. But it must do more than this. We are aiming to produce a curriculum which will be sufficiently basic and practical to be intelligible and stimulating to all our pupils, and not an intellectual minority who might, eventually, read the works of Cassirer and Hirst! Thus we must aim to incorporate a strand of culture which builds upon the everyday interests, the emerging career aspirations of our pupils. Finally, our common core cultural curriculum is not intended to serve as an instrument merely of induction and assimilation since we aim to encourage in our pupils those critical and creative dispositions from which new cultural and social possibilities will emerge. Thus, our core curriculum ought to include both (a) ways of identifying and analysing the principal features of culture which are of interest to us, educationally, and (b) a set of procedures for learning about, assessing, and modifying or reconstructing culture.

In Britain, the slow move towards a semi-universal system of comprehensive education provided a rare opportunity for thinking out and planning for a common core cultural curriculum. Individual schools have made some very interesting designs. Primary schools, too, have gained an opportunity to rethink their curriculum with the progressive abolition of the eleven-plus examination, but the most conspicuous achievements in that sector tend to be individualistic and activity-based. Conditions now exist, in both primary and secondary sectors, for individual schools to undertake, in a simple, practical way, cultural mapping.

Overall, this approach would result in a division of the curriculum into two parts, one of which is common to all pupils while the other provides opportunity for choice, specialisation and the pursuit of idiosyncratic and purely personal interests. From the cultural viewpoint, this second or optional part corresponds to the areas of choice and differentiation in culture, to those diverse interests and pursuits where people agree to differ or where choice need not imply any status differences. In present day secondary schools, examination syllabuses, hobbies and clubs, and special interest subjects would all come into the category of optionals.

This may cause some surprise. Are not the examination

subjects the staple of the curriculum and should not the school do all in its power to enable its pupils to satisfy their requirements? The answer to the first question is that they do form the staple, very often, even though not all pupils will take them, and, in the system as as a whole, a very substantial proportion will not. What is, in fact, a staple does not meet the needs of all of our pupils. The answer to the second question is: yes, schools ought to do everything possible to help examination pupils, everything, that is, consistent with an overall educational philosophy and organisation that acknowledges and provides for the needs of all pupils, irrespective of their academic talents.

But our concern, for the moment, is more with the common than with the special, individual aspects of the curriculum. How might this be outlined, as a set of cultural themes or broadly defined areas of experience? Much more work requires to be done in the field of culture analysis before a satisfactory answer can be given to this question. Something along the following lines might be considered as a starting point for school curriculum building. Studies would be conducted in:

(1) Typical work situations and modes of economic operation.
(2) Patterns of social meaning which include rules, norms of conduct, value systems and common social expectations.
(3) Introductions to and practical experience of the principal human symbolic systems of language, mathematics, science, history, religion, myth, the arts.
(4) Leisure and recreational interests and opportunities.
(5) Social and political institutions.
(6) Social and political policy.
(7) Styles of interpersonal relationships and ways of handling tension and conflict.
(8) Modes of individual expression and creativity.

This list is both schematic and incomplete. That is to say, it provides guidelines for the selection of curriculum content; it does not predetermine that content. It would be idle to pretend that an all-inclusive list could be agreed upon. In any case, schools do not need closed systems but indications of directions to follow. But schools also need more specific guidance in the way of themes, topics, and teaching and learning strategies. For each of the areas of human experience that we have listed we consider it important for curriculum development teams *outside* schools but including school teacher members, to create exemplary materials and strategies. The emphasis in these exemplars should be upon processes of enquiry and analysis and criticism, various forms of pupil engagement in practical, creative activities, and a general spirit of reflective action.

It would be altogether too easy to replace our existing curriculum by revamped content models clothed with information and pre-established viewpoints to be assimilated. What we are aiming to achieve is a personal engagement by pupils with the challenges, issues and problems posed for *them* within each of these major areas of experience. In this way, they can begin to participate in the mode of interpretation and acquire competency in tasks which are seen by them to be significant. To achieve this, teachers must learn to accept the personal and interpersonal character of knowledge itself, seeing it not as immutable, impersonal, and objective, but as the product of actions and enquiries engaged in by communities of thinkers and men of action. Unless knowledge is presented as problematic, a human achievement which as such is necessarily limited, partial and error-prone, pupils can hardly be expected to develop the confidence and self-assurance to take an active part in assessing and interpreting the realms of experience with which in the core curriculum they will be confronted.

Summary
We have pointed out the need for a national curriculum

125

policy which will include the broad outline and principal features of a common core cultural curriculum. This would enable all schools to provide a common core curriculum; one which is based on the different funds of experience and understanding available in our culture, which are not reducible to traditional 'subjects'. Approaches and methods are just as important as the content itself. There is no less a need for an analysis of teaching strategies that gets us beyond the now barren arguments between 'traditionalists' and 'progressives'. These strategies would relate to the modes of enquiry, interpretation and assessment which teachers and pupils will use in undertaking the cultural mapping which we have outlined. As with the map itself, these modes of enquiry cannot acquire a vivid, concrete reality until they are explored and worked out by practitioners in the schools.

Further reading
The issues here are complex and inevitably involve a wide range of reading. Hirst (1965), Hirst and Peters (1970), Chanan and Gilchrist (1974, Lawton (1975) and Skilbeck (1975) seem the minimum. It is worth making the effort to get access to a copy of Broudy, Smith and Burnett (1964).

Conclusion
Schools are entering a phase in which reaction against inadequately planned, over-ambitious curriculum innovations will be justifiably strong. But the need is for the better planning of curriculum reconstruction rather than less planning and curriculum inertia.

First, we must be clear what the possibilities open to schools really are. They can be summarised as follows:
(1) Schools can swim with the tide, identifying basic trends and features of culture and going along with rather than resisting them.

(2) Schools may identify particular values, beliefs and outlooks in the cultural heritage and seek to preserve them.

(3) Schools may largely ignore cultural trends and preserve some kind of island existence.

(4) Schools may set out to analyse, assess and think critically and creatively about their culture, looking for ways of contributing to its future development.

If teachers choose the fourth alternative, they have to be clear about what count as critical and creative contributions to the development of culture. There can be no such thing as conclusive 'proof' that a curriculum innovation will be for 'the better', any more than there can be 'proof' that existing practice is for the best.

The issue hinges on conceptions and valuations of culture which are so basic that in themselves they are not amenable to testing, for example by comparing curriculum results at one period of time or in a particular school with those of another. Suppose we take an apparently simple index of achievement, such as reading ability, and test the performance of large numbers of children of the same age group at different periods of time. It is true that the comparison may suggest whether an *average* child is a better reader or not, but it will only give us very crude indications of why particular groups of children in particular schools have done 'better' or 'worse'. However detailed and reliable the test results are, we still have to make judgements about the circumstances which are operating in particular schools.

Moreover, an evaluation that curriculum changes are for the better or worse hinges on agreement about what count as the most important aspects of children's learning. Because most people agree that reading is a crucial skill, it is easy to get consensus about it as the main criterion for judgement, even though an increase in reading ability might be obtained at the cost of other cultural skills, such as social sensibility.

But the case of reading ability is not typical of curriculum issues. More typically, changes have to be assessed within the wider context of what experiences have been forgone, what values given priority, what resources were available in the school. Such judgements are inescapably cultural valuations.

Cultural valuations are far more than matters of opinion when schools establish the social relationships and procedures through which a wide range of views and sources of feedback are taken into account. There is often a case for feasibility studies where the proposed changes are controversial or complex. It is more to the point that to consider curriculum construction in its cultural context is to *build in* procedures within the school for the appraisal of the need for change and the monitoring of the whole process of cultural mediation.

It is true that schools have little power to influence many of the social forces which impinge upon their work. But the scale of these changes only increases the obligation of schools to foster an active, reflective response to cultural change. The central curriculum resource here is the response of the teacher himself to cultural change: the example or model which he implicitly provides for children in his defining and resolution of practical curriculum dilemmas. We have suggested that this hinges on his disposition and ability to reinterpret basic conceptions and values. But this may not be enough unless ideas are articulated, evaluated and mobilised within a wider conception of rational curriculum planning. In turn this entails an understanding of the different dimensions of culture: social relations, symbolic forms, values and beliefs, ideology. Yet we cannot really claim to understand culture unless we can link detached reflection to cultural action itself. The most neglected aspect both of what we teach and of how we plan what we teach is the co-ordination of different forms of experience.

References and Name index

ADAMS, E. (1975) (ed.) *In-Service Education and Teachers' Centres.* Oxford, Pergamon. *102*

BAILEY, J. (1975) *Social Theory for Planning.* London, Routledge and Kegan Paul. *40*

BANKS, O. (1968) *The Sociology of Education.* London, Batsford. *33*

BANTOCK, G. H. (1968) *Culture, Industrialisation and Education.* London, Routledge and Kegan Paul. *70, 119*

BANTOCK, G. H. (1970) *Eliot and Education.* London, Faber. *32, 70*

BERGER, P. L. and LUCKMANN, T. (1967) *The Social Construction of Reality.* London, Allen Lane. *36*

BERNSTEIN, B. (1965) A sociolinguistic approach to social learning. In Gould (1965). *88*

BERNSTEIN, B. (1971) On the classification and framing of educational knowledge. In Young (1971). *36*

BOURDIEU, P. (1971) Systems of education and systems of thought. In Young (1971). *36, 37*

BROUDY, H. S., SMITH, B. O., and BURNETT, J. R. (1964) *Democracy and Excellence in American Secondary Education.* Chicago, Illinois, Rand McNally. *15, 126*

BROWN, R. (1973) *Education, Knowledge and Cultural Change.* London, Tavistock. *33*

BRUNER, J. S. (1960) *The Process of Education.* Cambridge, Mass., Harvard University Press. *7, 49*

BRUNER, J. S. (1966) *Toward a Theory of Instruction.* Cambridge, Mass., Harvard University Press. *49*

BRUNER, J. S. (1968) Culture, politics and pedagogy. *Saturday Review,* p. 69. Reprinted in Bruner (1974). *11, 29*

BRUNER, J. S. (1974) *The Relevance of Education.* London, Penguin Education. *47*

CASSIRER, E. (1944) *An Essay on Man.* Clinton, Mass., Yale University Press. *45*

CHANAN, G. and GILCHRIST, L. (1974) *What School Is For.* London, Methuen. *50, 121, 126*

CORBETT, P. (1965) *Ideologies.* London, Hutchinson. *86*

COX, C. B. and BOYSON, R. (1975) (eds) *Black Papers 1975.*

London, Dent. *75*

DAVIES, I. (1971) The managment of knowledge: a critique of the use of typologies in the sociology of education. In Young (1971). *36*

ELIOT T. S. (1948) *Notes Towards the Definition of Culture.* London, Faber and Faber. *32*

FICHTE, J. G. (1922) *Addresses to the German Nation* (trans. R. Jones and G. Turnbull). Chicago, Open Court. *66*

FREIRE, P. (1972a) *Pedagogy of the Oppressed.* New York, Herder and Herder. *84-6*

FREIRE, P. (1972b) *Cultural Action for Freedom.* London, Penguin. *84-6*

FREIRE, P. (1973) *Education for Critical Consciousness.* London, Sheed and Ward. *60, 83*

GOULD, J. (1965) (ed.) *Penguin Survey of Social Science.* Harmondsworth, Penguin.

HAMINGSON, D. (1973) (ed.) *Towards Judgement.* Norwich, University of East Anglia, Centre for Applied Research in Education. *53*

HARGREAVES. D. (1973) *Interpersonal Relations in Education.* London, Routledge and Kegan Paul. *36, 98*

HICKMAN, G. M., REYNOLDS, J. B. and TOLLEY, H. (1973) *A new Professionalism for a Changing Geography.* University of Bristol, for the Schools Council. *23*

HIRST, P. H. (1965) Liberal education and the nature of knowledge. In Archambault (1965). *49, 126*

HIRST, P. H. (1966) Educational theory. In Tibble (1966). *28*

HIRST, P. H. (1975) *Knowledge and the Curriculum.* London, Routledge and Kegan Paul. *62*

HIRST, P. H. and PETERS, R. S. (1970) *The Logic of Education.* London, Routledge and Kegan Paul. *49, 121, 126*

HOGGART, R. (1973) *Speaking to Each Other,* Volume 1: *About Society.* Harmondsworth, Penguin. *47*

HOPPER, E. (1973) Educational systems and consequences of mobility. In Brown (1973). *33*

HOYLE, E. (1972) See The Open University (1972). *112*

HUMANITIES CURRICULUM PROJECT (1970) *The Humanities Project: an Introduction.* London, Heinemann Educational. *73*

INGLIS, F. (1975) *Ideology and the Imagination.* London, Cambridge University Press. *10*

JACKSON, P. W. (1968) *Life in Classrooms.* New York, Holt, Rinehart and Winston. *34*

JENKINS, D. (1975) See The Open University (1975). *11*

JENKINS, D. and RAGGATT, P. (1974) See The Open University (1974). *115*

KEDDIE, N. (1971) Classroom Knowledge. In Young (1971). *36*

KEDDIE, N. (1973) *Tinker, Tailor . . . the Myth of Cultural Depriva-tion*. Harmondsworth, Penguin. *88*

KELLER, H. (1902) *The Story of My Life*. New York, Doubleday. *46*

KROEBER A. L. and KLUCKHOHN, C. (1952) Culture: a crit-ical review of concepts and definitions. *Papers of the Peabody Museum of Archaeology and Ethnology*, **47**. *26*

LAWTON, D. (1973) *Social Change, Educational Theory and Cur-riculum Planning*. London, University of London Press. *15, 19, 21, 23, 60*

LAWTON, D. (1975) *Class, Culture and the Curriculum*. London, Routledge and Kegan Paul. *15, 78, 126*

MAGEE, B. (1973) *Popper*. London, Fontana/Collins. *62*

MEDAWAR, P. B. (1969) *The Art of the Soluble*. Harmondsworth, Penguin Books. *57*

MIDWINTER, E. (1972) *Projections* and *Social Environment and the Urban School*. London, Ward Lock. *11*

MOORE, T. W. (1974) *Educational Theory: an Introduction*. London, Routledge and Kegan Paul. *28*

MUSGRAVE, P. W. (1973) *Knowledge, Curriculum and Change*. London, Angus and Robertson. *36*

NASH, R. (1973) *Classrooms Observed*. London, Routledge and Kegan Paul. *34*

NYERERE, J. (1973) *Freedom and Development: Writings and Speeches 1968-1973*. Oxford, Clarendon Press. *85*

ORTEGA Y GASSET, J. (1959) *Man and Crisis*. London, Allen and Unwin. *54*

PHENIX, P. H. (1964) *Realms of Meaning*. New York, McGraw-Hill. *121*

POSTMAN, N. and WEINGARTNER, C. (1969) *Teaching as a Subversive Activity*. New York, Delacorte Press. *44*

REID, W. A. and WALKER, D. F. (1975) *Case Studies in Curriculum Change*. London, Routledge and Kegan Paul. *36*

RENNIE, J., LUNZER, E. A. and WILLIAMS, W. T. (1974) *Social Education: an Experiment in Four Secondary Schools*. Schools Council Working Paper 51. London, Evans/Methuen. *15*

RICHARDSON, E. (1975) *Authority and Organisation in the Secondary School*. London, Macmillan Educational. *29, 98, 112*

ROSEN, H. (1972) *Language and Class: a Critical Look at the Theories of Basil Bernstein*. Bristol, Falling Wall Press. *57, 88*

SCHOOLS COUNCIL (1965) *Change and Response*. London, H.M.S.O. *105*

SCHOOLS COUNCIL (1973) *Pattern and Variation in Curriculum Development*. London, Macmillan. *106*

SCHOOLS COUNCIL (1975) *Working Paper 53: The Whole Cur-riculum*. London, Evans/Methuen. *120*

SCHWAB, J. (1969) The practical: a language for curriculum. *School Review*, **79**, No. 4. *21*

SHAW, K. E. (1975) Negotiating curriculum change in a college of education. In Reid and Walker (1975). *36*

SHIPMAN, M. D. (1968) *The Sociology of the School*. London, Longmans, Green and Co. *34*

SHIPMAN, M. D. (1974) *Inside a Curriculum Project*. London, Methuen. *98*

SKILBECK, M. (1970) *John Dewey*. London, Collier-Macmillan. *19*

SKILBECK, M. (1975) See The Open University (1975). *49, 75, 121, 126*

SMITH, B. O., STANLEY, W. O. and SHORES, J. H. (1957) *Fundamentals of Curriculum Development*. New York, Harcourt, Brace and World. *4*

STENHOUSE, L. (1967) *Culture and Education*. London, Nelson. *51*

STENHOUSE, L. (1975) *An Introduction to Curriculum Research and Development*. London, Heinemann. *11, 109, 115*

SUTTON, C. R. and HAYSOM, J. T. (1974) *The Art of the Science Teacher*. London, McGraw-Hill. *63*

TAWNEY, D. A. (1974) The nature of science and scientific enquiry. In Sutton and Haysom (1974). *62*

THE OPEN UNIVERSITY (1972) *Problems of Curriculum Innovation*. Course E283, Units 13-14 (by E. Hoyle). Milton Keynes, The Open University Press.

THE OPEN UNIVERSITY (1974) *Alternatives for Urban Schools*. Course E351, Block 5 (by D. Jenkins and P. Raggatt). Milton Keynes, The Open University Press.

THE OPEN UNIVERSITY (1975) E203 *Curriculum Design and Development*. Milton Keynes, The Open University Press. *112 Ideology, Knowledge and the Curriculum*. Units 3 and 4 (by M. Skilbeck and A. Harris).

Man: a Course of Study. Units 14-15, Part 1 (by D. Jenkins).

THOMPSON, K. and WHITE, J. (1975) *Curriculum Development: a Dialogue*. London, Pitman. *115*

TOULMIN, S. (1972) *Human Understanding*, Volume I: *The Collective Use and Evolution of Concepts*. Oxford, Clarendon Press. *62*

TYLER, R. W. (1949) *Basic Principles of Curriculum and Instruction*. Chicago, University of Chicago Press. *21, 29*

TYLOR, E. B. (1871) *Primitive Culture*. London, John Murray. *26*

WHITE, J. (1973) *Towards a Compulsory Curriculum*. London, Routledge and Kegan Paul. *15*

WILLIAMS, R. (1950) *Culture and Society 1780-1950*. London, Chatto and Windus. *58*

YOUNG, M. F. D. (1971) (ed.) *Knowledge and Control*. New York, Collier-Macmillan. *36*

132

Subject index